Mental Manipulation

The Defense Guide Against Persuasion

Tactics, Covert Mind Games, and

Emotional Control

VICTOR SYKES

Table of Contents

Recognize Emotional Manipulation in Relationships 84

INTRODUCTION

Do you ever feel like you are being manipulated? Do you feel like others somehow seem to have an unseen power over you? Are you unsure of whether you are being manipulated or not? If your answer to these questions is "yes," then this is the perfect book for you.

I want to thank you for purchasing this book, *Mental Manipulation*, and hope it helps you understand how people manipulate us, and how we can stand our ground and take control of our lives.

There might have been different instances in your life when either you were manipulated into doing or not doing something, or when you used manipulation to get someone else to do or not do something. So, what is acceptable and what isn't acceptable? For instance, if a parent uses manipulation to get their child to eat vegetables, it is acceptable, but if a partner uses manipulation to coerce you into doing something that you aren't comfortable with, that's not okay!

So, you need to learn the difference between acceptable and unacceptable forms of manipulation and how you can recognize any form of mental manipulation. If you don't want to find yourself in situations that harm you in any way, ones that you know you could have avoided by simply standing your ground, then you need to learn to work around mental manipulation.

In this book, you will learn the different aspects of mental manipulation, the common techniques that manipulators use, how you can recognize if you are being manipulated, and tips to overcome such manipulation. Apart from this, you will also learn about the different types of manipulation and the acceptable ways in which you can use them.

If you are ready to learn more, then let us get started immediately.

BONUS!

As an additional 'thank you' for reading this book, I want to give you another book for free. The book is:

The Simple and Powerful Word to Use to Increase Your Social Status

It's a quick read that will add a powerful tool to your psychological toolbox.

Follow the link below and you can claim the book instantly.

Click Here for Instant Access!

or go to VictorSykes.com/free-ebook

CHAPTER ONE

About Manipulation

What is Mental Manipulation?

Manipulation is not something that is ever considered to be a positive form of influence. Psychological manipulation is a form of social control in which one makes use of the mental and emotional vulnerabilities of a person. It is a tactic that enables a person to use someone else's weakness as an effective weapon against them. Psychological manipulation often changes the perception as well as the behavior of others. It includes the application of certain tactics that are deceptive, underhanded and, at times, abusive. Such methods are not only devious and deceptive but are exploitative.

Manipulation gives a certain degree of control to the manipulator over the person being manipulated. It tends to apply different forms of psychological abuse, emotional blackmail, coercion, or even bullying to get others to do things that they might not do naturally.

Why do People Manipulate?

Different things like pathological lying, smear campaigns, love bombings, and even bullying are all forms of manipulation. Before you learn more about these various forms, we need to look into why some people resort to manipulation—what makes people use manipulation instead of being their authentic selves?

At the heart of it, manipulation is about the feelings of worthlessness and fear. What makes a person resort to using manipulative tactics to secure a specific behavior or action? The most obvious answer to this question is fear. The simple fear that, as things are, the person will not be able to generate the desired result based solely on their merits; that life in general, as well as their peers, will not react favorably to them. Manipulators also tend to believe that everything that they're connected to is positioned unfavorably to them and is against them.

They fear that others are capable of doing things that they cannot, and that there are scarce resources in this "dog eat dog" world, and that they need to resort to manipulation to preserve themselves—financially, practically or even emotionally. Manipulators tend to have this fear of, "What will happen if I don't make this happen?" Or, "Will I willingly let anyone else have the upper hand over me if I don't use manipulation?"

Now it is time to dig deeper into the mind of a manipulator.

Fear is the primary motivator that leads to manipulation, and it comes from a person's belief that they are not worthy. This roughly translates into, "I am not worthy of life working favorably for me, and I am not worthy of everything else (life and people) having my best interests at heart."

Manipulation is also about the lack of a conscious. This lack of consciousness occurs when a person doesn't realize that they—and nobody else—are responsible for their reality. Being unconscious of this reality tends to establish a direct correlation between the events in their life and the internal feeling of beingness. So, what does this correlation even mean? It simply says that they don't believe in the system of, "as within, as without." A person who is devoid of consciousness doesn't believe that such a system exists in spite of the repetition in patterns, any painful episodes, and reoccurring disappointments.

They don't learn from their previous experiences and don't understand that the inner emotions they feel are directly proportional to the outer life that they experience; they do not evolve and do not understand it. They feel that the world is unsafe and that the only way in which they can attain the results that they desire is by manipulation, and this brings them right back where they started, over and over again. Manipulators try to eliminate this pain and, to do so, need to create another manipulation.

Does manipulation have any long-lasting results or is it just a quick fix? It is nothing more than a quick fix since it is not an authentic or genuine action. Instead, it is more of a defensive reaction that stems from negative feelings and beliefs.

Manipulation is a deliberate action, and it is not in sync with the consciousness of thoughts of any greater good. A manipulator's lack of understanding of the role he plays in the bigger picture and lack of any self-realization leads to all this. Whenever someone is trying to gain through manipulation instead of authenticity, the results they attain aren't authentic, and this vicious cycle goes on.

Anything that one gains from such a level of unconsciousness can only create victories that are hollow, leads to emptiness and, of course, makes the manipulator feel more unworthy than ever. This feeling tends to separate them from all that is good in life.

Being unaware means not learning, not evolving, and feeling unworthy. Therefore, only those who truly feel unworthy at the core of their being are the ones who resort to manipulation.

Common Expressions of Manipulation

To further understand the concept of manipulation, there is one other thing that we should understand—the manipulators are not just the ones who are lacking in conscience.

You might know—and might have also experienced—the lengths that a narcissist might go to manipulate and secure a supply of extreme agendas.

Let us take a look at a rather interesting scenario to understand more about manipulation:

A couple has been together for over a year, and one partner admits that, due to her fear of abandonment, she always has this need to ensure that her partner always "needs" her. Does this make her manipulative? Before you start feeling bad for her, let me answer this question. Yes, it makes her manipulative, and her acts are a means of avoiding dealing with her issues. Instead of working on her fear of being abandoned, she resorts to manipulation. This is not fair to either of the partners since their relationship is not based on authenticity. A manipulator doesn't necessarily have to be a narcissist; they can be loving, caring, and have high levels of integrity. Some form of conditioning that she was exposed to has made her conclude that to be loved she must be needed. So, she truly believes that if someone stops needing her, they will stop loving her as well. This is nothing but a misconception, and it comes from her lack of understanding that everyone is worthy of love, and being loved, for being their authentic selves.

Manipulation stems from people's negative beliefs of themselves, of those around them, and their lives in general.

CHAPTER TWO

About Manipulation and Persuasion

Psychological manipulation is a self-serving attempt that a manipulator makes beyond their competence to elicit a specific behavior from the other person (manipulator's victim) on a particular matter.

Difference between Manipulation and Influence or Persuasion

When you call someone manipulative, it is often a criticism. If you say that you are being manipulated, then that's a complaint against the treatment you are receiving.

Manipulation is a dodgy concept at best and immoral at worst. Why is this? Why is manipulation undesirable? Human beings tend to manipulate each other in different ways, and most of us tend to do it unknowingly. What differentiates manipulation from influencing and why is it undesirable?

Almost all of us are regularly subjected to some attempt at manipulation. The gaslighting technique is often used to plant a seed of doubt in someone, so that they start to question their judgment and, instead, decide to rely on the manipulator's advice. Guilt tripping is when someone makes you feel guilty about doing or not doing something that the manipulator desires of you. Peer pressure can force someone to care too much about the manipulator's approval, so that they do what the manipulator wants them to.

Advertisements actively try to manipulate viewers by encouraging them to form false beliefs. For instance, when the advertisements portray fried chicken as a healthy food or encourage faulty associations—as when cigarettes are wrongly associated with the rugged vigor of masculinity—we have manipulation.

Phishing and other similar scams try to manipulate their victims by using some method of deception, playing on basic emotions like greed, fear or even sympathy.

Then, there are other instances of manipulation that are rather straightforward—for instance, a popular example of manipulation is when Iago successfully manipulates Othello and plants seeds of doubt about Desdemona's fidelity by preying on his uncertainties and making him jealous. It works him up into a murderous rage, so much so that he murders his beloved.

Mental Manipulation

Manipulation is probably wrong since it harms the victim. At times, if it is successful—such as with a manipulative cigarette ad—it can even cause death or a dreadful disease. Manipulative scams like phishing lead to identity theft and fraud; social manipulation can result in abusive and toxic relationships.

However, manipulation isn't always harmful. At times, manipulation is even desirable. For instance, let us assume that an individual has just gone through a breakup and is out of a toxic relationship, but in a moment of weakness, she wants to go back to her abusive partner. Now, imagine that her friends start to use a technique that's similar to the one that Iago used on Othello. The friends are trying to manipulate her into a fit of rage that will discourage her from resuming a toxic relationship. If this kind of manipulation prevents her from any form of reconciliation, then she will certainly be better off than she would've been had her friends not manipulated her. To many, this might seem a little sketchy, morally.

There is something that is still morally undecided about manipulation, even when it helps. So, if you use harm as a criterion to define manipulation, then it isn't right.

Perhaps manipulation is considered to be wrong because it uses techniques that are immoral based on the way it treats others. This idea might be quite appealing to those who believe that morality is essential and that we must treat each other as rational beings instead of objects. The only right way to influence someone else's behavior is through rational persuasion, and anything that doesn't fit in the definition of rational persuasion is undesirable. Even this answer tends to fall short; for all intents and purposes, it will condemn even those forms of influence that are morally well-intentioned.

For instance, the manipulative tactic that Iago used was to appeal to Othello's feelings and emotions. Emotional appeal isn't manipulative at all times. Moral persuasion often appeals to certain emotions like empathy, or at least it tries to convey how it will feel to have others do something that you are doing to them.

Likewise, if you get someone to fear that a specific thing or act is dangerous or even harmful, then to experience guilt for doing this might not seem fair. Even an invitation to doubt one's judgment is not necessarily manipulative in situations where there is a good reason to do so. All forms of non-rational influence don't necessarily have to be manipulative in nature.

So, what is the difference between influence and manipulation? It might seem like there is a fine line to tread between these two. The only difference is the intent with which either is used. Iago's actions were certainly manipulative, and even evil, since he intended to make Othello think in the wrong way. Iago was fully aware of the fact that Othello did not have a reason to be jealous, but he led him to believe it anyway. This is a form of emotional manipulation that's similar to deceptive ways used by Iago to trick Othello into forming such beliefs that Iago knows are false to begin with. Emotional gaslighting takes place when the manipulator tricks the victim into doubting what the manipulator believes to be good judgment.

In contrast, advising an angry friend to prevent them from making any rash judgments before calming down is not manipulative, provided you are aware of the fact that your friend's ability to think rationally is temporarily switched off.

If a conman tries to make you feel empathetic toward a non-existent African prince, he is clearly manipulating you to elicit a pure emotion—like empathy—for someone who doesn't even exist. On the other hand, if someone tries to make you feel empathetic toward the suffering of people who are real and the appeal is sincere, then it results in moral persuasion and not manipulation. For instance, if someone starts a fund-raising drive to help all those affected by a terrible natural disaster, then their tactics amount to moral persuasion and not manipulation. If an abusive and unfaithful person tries to make their partner feel bad or guilty for raising any suspicions about their fidelity, then such an act is manipulation because the abusive partner is preying on the victim's misplaced guilt. However, if a friend tries to make you feel guilty for abandoning her in her time of need, then that's not manipulative—that's just a means of making you understand how your acts affected her.

There is a common characteristic that makes influencing and manipulation morally wrong—the manipulator tries to get the victim to adopt what the manipulator knows to be a wrong belief or emotion. In this manner, manipulation is quite similar to lying. The factor that makes a statement a lie and morally wrong is one in the same—the speaker trying to get the victim to believe what the speaker knows to be an immoral belief.

In both these instances, the person exuding influence intends to induce the victim into believing something wrong or inducing them to make a mistake. The liar will try to make you believe something to be untrue and, therefore, enable you to form a wrong belief. The manipulator certainly does what the liar does, but apart from this, the manipulator will also make the victim feel an inappropriate emotion (doubting and misjudging someone else, feeling weak or unworthy, and so on) that's completely baseless.

The main difference between manipulation and any other form of non-manipulative influence depends on whether the person exuding the influence is tricking someone into making a mistake. Manipulation trickles down to immorality. The manipulator does it with the knowledge that they are leading the victim down the wrong path— they're trying to deceive the victim into believing something that the manipulator knows isn't true.

It is a primary trait of the human race that we all influence each other in different ways, apart from rational persuasion. At times, influencing can help improve a person's decision-making ability by leading them to believe, critically analyze things, or even encourage them to pay attention to the right things. At times, influence can also throw a spanner in the works by leading someone to pay attention to the wrong things, or even by discouraging them. Manipulation involves the deliberate use of influence to hamper a person's ability to make the right decision, and that's the reason why manipulation is immoral.

So, when your heart is in the right place, and you have good intentions while exuding a little influence on someone else, and you know that this influence will help the other person to make a good decision, then that's not manipulation; however, don't just assume that you always know best. For instance, if your friend is drunk and is intent on calling up his ex, and you know that it's a bad idea and you discourage it, then it isn't manipulation—it is persuasion, and you can let your friend decide for himself once he sobers up. You will learn more about different forms of manipulation, the common tactics used, and the ways to spot manipulative tactics in the coming chapter.

CHAPTER THREE

Traits of Manipulative People

Manipulators have mastered the art of deception. They might seem quite sincere and even respectable, but that's nothing more than a façade they keep up for the sake of appearance. Only when they draw you in and know that they have trapped you, do they reveal their true colors.

Manipulators are not interested in you and only think of you as a means of attaining the ends that they desire. So, you unwittingly become a pawn in their game. The worst thing is that you aren't aware of the rules of the game and they keep changing them to fit their needs. They do this in different ways, and if you pay a little attention, then you will be able to see through them. They will often use your words against you; they will twist your words in such a way that the words become unrecognizable to you. Manipulators will try to confuse you and might even make you believe that you are crazy. Distorting the truth and lying are the two things that are always present in a manipulator's arsenal.

Manipulators tend to play the victim card quite well and will make you seem like you are the one that caused all the trouble. They will make you the scapegoat, and you won't even notice it. They can seem passive aggressive one moment, or even nice, and then seem standoffish the very next second. They will encourage you to second-guess yourself and will prey on all your fears and insecurities without any remorse. They also tend to make you quite defensive. Manipulators can be vicious, aggressive, and can also resort to personal attacks to get what they want, bullying and threatening to get their way.

Traits of Manipulators

In this section, you will learn about the different traits that manipulators exhibit. If you can understand these traits, that will help you understand the way they think and operate. Once you get the hang of it, then you will be able to spot a manipulator from a mile away, and it will help you stay alert. So, if you are ready, let's learn about the basic traits of a manipulative person.

Manipulators tend to lack insight about the way in which they engage with others and end up making up scenarios, or they honestly believe that their way of dealing with a situation is the only right way to go about it to meet their needs. After all, the only thing that matters for them is to get their way. Ultimately, all situations are always about them, and it doesn't matter to them what others think, feel, or even want.

Manipulators don't understand what boundaries mean. They are quite resilient in the pursuit of their goals, and they have little or even no regard for who gets hurt in the process. Crossing your boundaries—physical, emotional, psychological, or even spiritual ones, is not their concern.

They don't understand what personal space is and even if they do, they don't care. They are quite similar to parasites, and these examples of behavior are acceptable. But when it comes to human behavior, having someone else leeching off you is not a good thing, and it is exhausting.

Manipulators tend to shrug off all responsibilities for their acts and instead blame others for causing them to behave the way they do. It doesn't mean that a manipulator doesn't understand what responsibility means; they understand it well. The problem is that they don't see anything wrong with shrugging off responsibility for their actions and will make others assume this responsibility. Ultimately, they aim to try to pass off the responsibility onto others to fulfill their needs, and, in this process, they will not leave any room for you to fulfill yours.

They tend to prey on other's sensibilities, emotions, and conscientiousness. They know that they have a good chance of reeling you in because you are a kind and caring person who wants to help. They might seem good and kind initially, and will even praise you for the work that you do.

After a while, you will notice that the praise stops. This happens because a manipulator doesn't care about anyone except themselves. All they care about is what they can get others to do for them and not the other way around.

If you want to differentiate manipulators from those who are empathetic, then you need to pay close attention to the way that they speak about others concerning you. If they are capable of talking ill about people behind their backs, then don't put it past them to talk ill about you behind your back. Manipulators will often try to degrade someone else to make you feel better about yourself. They are adept at triangulation and will create such situations that allow all sorts of negative emotions to creep in.

You must never waste any of your precious time trying to explain who you are to those who cannot understand you. If someone doesn't understand you, then there is no point in waiting around until they do.

Never wait around for a manipulator to like or understand you.

Manipulators always tend to present themselves differently to different people—they are like chameleons. If they believe that they need to be a certain way to win someone over, then they will do so, and they tend to exhibit different personas when they are with different people—it almost feels like they are different people altogether. For instance, a manipulator might say that they like to swim to get close to someone and then criticize the same thing when they are with someone else.

Facts about Manipulators and Manipulation

Throughout your life, you will come across potholes and sinkholes that are deliberately placed by manipulators. Manipulation can stem from an individual, a group, a company, organization, or even the government. Regardless of whom it is coming from, certain facts hold true.

Manipulators will:

- always present the information in such a manner that you will be forced to believe that it is helpful and it is something that you need, even when it does nothing for you

- make you believe that if something is repeated over and over again, then it must be true

- never want you to investigate or even consider things from a standpoint that's different from theirs

- try to instigate an immediate, negative reaction to ideas that are different from theirs, and will be quick to disregard any such ideas

- try to keep you dependent on them for as long as they possibly can

- try to keep you thoroughly engaged so that you don't have the time to stay in tune with your spirit

- not want you to become fully aware of your gut feeling, and they like to believe that they know best

- encourage you to concentrate more on feeling good instead of being good

- bombard you with a lot of distracting information so that you don't concentrate on what they do or say

- never help you focus on the things that you can learn from the success and failures of others

- want you to work with the information that they supply even when it isn't of benefit to you

- help you to become comfortable in a fake safety-net instead of encouraging you to do better in life

- often label critical thinking and any form of analytical thinking as negative and undesirable behaviors

- often derive more benefits from their supposed "assistance" than you ever will

- always try to take advantage of you

- try to destroy whomever comes in their way and who wants to reveal the truth. To do this, they will use different diversionary tactics—character assassination is their go-to tool for this purpose. If they destroy a person's credibility, then no one will believe such a person—mission accomplished!

- never take any responsibility

- tend to use sympathy, tears, and other emotions to victimize themselves.

- want you to choose frequent entertainment over maturity

- always try to get you to believe their words more than their actions

- need you to believe that they are the absolute authority on a topic (regardless of whether they are or not) so that their beliefs will become a point of reference for you and the only acceptable truth

- shamelessly prey on your emotions without any form of remorse or guilt

- want you to reach a decision or a conclusion based solely on the information that they supply. The information that they supply will only be from their perspective and not from anyone else's

- try to engage you with different things so that you don't have the time to think about anything specific

- never to let you be independent. They like to feel needed

- always want you to choose their choices instead of believing that you are capable of coming to your conclusions. This is one thing that a manipulator will try to avoid at all costs

- want you to be more head-centered and not spirit-oriented

- want you to stay limited for them to like or accept you

- not do anything to appreciate or even strengthen your knowledge about anything

- try to confuse you by bombarding you with information that they know you cannot verify

- use opposite words while conversing. For instance, they might say something like, "I respect your opinion, but you are a fool." Such statements will make you doubt yourself even when you are of clear mind about the subject or situation

CHAPTER FOUR

Ways in Which People Try to Manipulate You

In this chapter, we will look at the most common ways in which bullies make you do their will. These signs are all too common with most manipulators and, after reading these, you will likely relate these traits to one or more people in your life.

Acting Superior

Some individuals may seem quite arrogant, who often tend to act like they are somehow superior to you. Maybe they are under the false notion that acting superior to others makes them feel more adult-like and that you are more of a child. This superior and inferior attitude is a sign of manipulation. For this strategy to work well, you will need to give into the manipulator's wishes. To combat this, be aware that no one is superior to you and you aren't inferior to anyone. Don't let anyone talk down to you. If someone is doing this, it is only because you are allowing them to.

Condescending Remarks

Sometimes people try to talk to you in a condescending or contemptuous tone, trying to belittle you by saying things like, "Don't be stupid" or "You're being ridiculous."

These are not just indulgent remarks and will be delivered in a manipulative tone. Actors often use whispering to achieve a dramatic effect, as if revealing some secret; influencers, persecutors, and sales associates often use very targeted, specific vocabulary and tone to establish mutual understanding and to influence others.

Jokes that Aren't Funny

No, I am not putting down those with a bad sense of humor. Instead, I am talking about a common tactic that manipulators use.

Another common tactic that is frequently used by manipulators is to joke at your expense, especially when others are around.

This likely occurs over the internet through social media, or trying to humiliate you in front of others, making fun of how you walk and talk, or, in worst cases, about things you cannot control—for instance, anything to do with your eyes, face, height, nose or color of skin; none of which are funny.

"Sticks and stones will break your bones, but words will never hurt you."

Well, words hurt more than punches thrown. Barbed words and jaded comments cause more damage than a physical blow. Worse yet, if you get angry and ask the manipulator what their problem is, they will often try to protect their behavior by saying they are "joking" or "having fun." They may even add insult to injury, saying that you are "too sensitive" or "too delicate." They can even offer sincere apologies to silence you to keep you from complaining—"I am sorry that you felt that way."

Dirty Looks

Sometimes, an image or a facial expression draws a thousand words without the person uttering a single syllable.

Be wary of any of the following aggressive and intimidating facial expressions that are used to try to frighten and force you to withdraw and surrender:

- indulgent inclination of the head
- degrading look through glasses

- dirty looks and looks of death

- prolonged eye contact, without blinking or saying anything

- blank eyes

- looks like anger, disgust, hatred, hostility, condemnation, outrage, etc.

- raising an eyebrow

- shaking head

- smiling, winking, condescending, or arrogant looks that say, "I know something you don't know" or "I'm smarter than you"

Bullying

Why do people like to intimidate or bully others? Because it works. Most people are afraid of conflict and confrontation, and will do everything possible to avoid them. This is where bullies thrive.

All a bully needs is to begin to behave in an aggressive, hostile, and threatening manner, and create the impression that others have to tread on eggshells around them, combining body language, facial expressions, and tonality, in order to send a clear message of, "Don't you dare mess with me or you'll regret it!"

As a result, the majority avoid them for fear of hostility, or they tend to suck up to them in a bid to be in their good books.

Intimidation tactics aren't just physical. At school, a bully can use his size and the threat of physical violence to intimidate you. At work, your manager may try to intimidate you directly or indirectly, threatening the safety of your job if you don't do what they want you to do— examples being working holidays, weekends or extra hours without additional charge, or doing something that is not part of the job description.

Physical Intimidation

If someone is significantly bigger, taller or stronger than you are, then they can try to use their physical size to dominate, intimidate, or threaten you, especially if you are small in stature. However, there is one thing that you can do to protect yourself—it might sound a little radical, but it is a good idea to learn some form of self-defense; you never know when it might come in handy. If you are scared or worried about your safety, don't hesitate to call the police.

If bullying occurs at home, you should contact your Human Resources department immediately. It is not okay for anyone to physically threaten you.

A Raised Voice

"Do not raise your voice, improve your arguments." - Desmond Tutu

Shouting is a commonly used aggressive tactic to harass and control you.

Rather than improving their arguments, many will alter their volume and start to shout to get their point across. In extreme cases, yelling and screaming will be used to control the conversation and bully you. If someone starts shouting or yelling at you, or speaks much louder than necessary, stay calm and encourage them to do so non-aggressively, without emotion. In a majority of cases, this confuses the manipulator, and they become very shy and uncomfortable and immediately lower their voice.

Silent Treatment

One of the most favored tactics is the silent treatment, in the hope that you will eventually approach or contact the manipulator.

Playing Hard to Get

This is similar to the tactic of acting condescending. By playing hard to get, the manipulator is trying to make you feel like you are inferior to them.

Beware of anyone who tries any of the following tactics on you:

- The person recognizes everyone in the room but is making it a point to leave you feeling ignored.

- Acting bored/disinterested/uncomfortable whenever you try to talk to them or initiate a conversation.

- The person doesn't respond to any of your comments, questions, emails or any other form of communication and always seems to be "very busy" whenever you need to talk to them.

- Tends to leave the room as soon as you enter.

- Tries to avoid all eye contact with you whenever you are talking to them.

- Refuses to acknowledge your existence.

In fact, this seems like a scene straight out of the movie "Mean Girls" when the popular girls—the plastics—avoid all those whom they thought weren't "cool" enough for them.

My advice to you is, if people ignore you, you need to ignore it. If they step back from you, take ten steps back farther. Or, if you need to talk to them, call them and ask them what their problem is. Sometimes, it is better to confront them and get it over with instead of wondering what is it that you did to deserve such treatment.

Guilt Tripping

This is perhaps the most favorite pastime of manipulators and usually arises when a victim doesn't do what the manipulator expects, and so the manipulator will use phrases similar to these to make the victim feel guilty:

"I thought we were friends."

"I thought I could count on you."

"I cannot believe how selfish you are!"

"I've always been with you, and now you cannot even lift a finger to help me?"

Victimization

Acting like a martyr and the "poor me" attitude:

"I'm very busy, and yet you expect me to do this?"

"I have a lot of work, and you want me to help you around the house?"

"I cannot do anything right, and I always make a mess of things!"

"Nothing I do is good enough!"

Playing with Emotions

Some people are teachers of emotional manipulation and are not shy when it comes to playing with their emotions to get what they want. They will tell you that they love you, they will tell you that they hate you, or they will try to make you angry, sad or jealous; it does not matter—anything to get what they want.

Advertisers and, in particular, the media are the main masters of emotional manipulation. They know that if they can make you feel something, they can make you do something. So instead of wasting time trying to convince you logically, they manipulate you emotionally with images and footage of cute—or suffering—kids and animals; everything they need to achieve the desired result. This is a lousy trick, but it's effective, and it works!

Approval, Approval, and more Approval

Another favorite tactic of manipulators is conditional approval: You get support, love, help, sex, etc. if you give them what they want.

This tactic works only if you have the habit of seeking the approval of others and if that approval matters to you. When you seek approval from others, you give them power over you and give them the opportunity to manipulate your feelings and make you feel worthless anytime they want. In other words, you are becoming a slave to their opinions.

Remember, what others can give you, they can also take. If they can lift you, they can also break you. And what if you are looking for someone's approval and he refuses to give it? What are you going to do then? To try? Do you feel like you are worthless?

If someone doesn't take you for who you are or treat you the way they would like to be treated, release them.

Time Limits

False time limits are often used to pressure you and do not give you time to think.

Bosses often use false time limits to manipulate their employees:

- "We have a timeline!"
- "The client is waiting!"
- "We do not have time to discuss it!"
- "This is urgent! You cannot go home until it's done! "

Companies often use fake time limits to boost sales:

- "ONLY TODAY! Up to 50% off!"
- "Closing the sale! Be quick or lose out!"

Employers give potential employees false time limits to join:

- "You have 48 hours to accept this offer, or it will be withdrawn."

There is a reason why people use false time limits: Sellers know that "time kills transactions" and the more time you have to think and weigh all your options, the less likely you are to do what you should do. They just want you to buy their product or service.

Free Lunch

A clever trick of manipulators is to offer you a gift, or a "free" service, or something you did not ask for, and then ask for something in return:

- "Free evaluation"

- "Free"

- "No obligation, free quotation."

But, know that there is no such thing as a free lunch or something for nothing. When someone gives you something, they almost always want something in return. Maybe it's money, time, advice, help or service. If you're in doubt, ask them, find out what they want in return, because there is almost always a hidden agenda.

Some people are very kind and try to influence/ convince/ manipulate/ give compliments and praise when trying to flatter and conquer. Everything they say is like music to your ears. Instead of telling you the truth, they are trying to seem favorable to you and will say things that they think you want to hear. This is an intelligent tactic because everyone likes to receive compliments, to be approved of and hear nice things said about them—compliments are one of the quickest ways to establish mutual understanding, make new friends, and get someone to reduce their protection.

Sweet-talkers know that when they make you feel good, you most likely want to repay the favor by doing something good to make them feel good. Also, let's be honest, the more you love someone (your best friend, partner, children), the easier it is for them to manipulate you.

Loaded Questions

Loaded questions are questions made with an unfair assumption incorporated in them—often with a presumption of guilt. They are often asked to try to put you on the back foot.

For example:

- "Why are you still lying?"
- "Why do not you admit that you stole it?"
- "Why do not you admit you're wrong?"

The initial questions suggest an answer to a question in an attempt to catch it. They are often asked by lawyers in court:

- "Do you still have an addiction to the game?"
- "Why are you lying?"

Neglected self-help sellers often try to manipulate the audience into seminars, asking important questions to catch them when buying their products:

- "Are you a talker or a doer?"

- "Are you a winner or a loser?"

- "Do you want to be rich or poor?"

Altered Perceptions

Some people will try to poison your perception of others before they've even met them, saying something bad about them, so you doubt and don't trust them:

- "I would not trust him, everything he says is a lie!"

- "I know she looks cute, but you must be careful because she;'s a user and a bitch!"

Politicians and the media are known to poison the well and try to destroy the reputation of people they do not like with gossip, rumors, and defamatory tactics. During the 2016 presidential campaign, Donald Trump called his opponents:

- "Hillary Curve"

- "Mad Bernie"

- "Small frame"
- "Low Energy Jeb"
- "Lying Ted"

My advice is to not let anyone change your perception of anyone in a negative manner or to plant doubt in your mind and dictate it.

Decide for yourself.

Fear of Fear

"People respond to fear, not love; they don't teach that in Sunday School, but it's true." Richard Nixon, the 37th President of the United States.

Fighting fear is another extremely powerful weapon, which is why publicists, politicians, religions such as Christianity and Islam, and the media (the greatest of all those who fear it) use it so often.

Fighting fear may be obvious or elusive, but it is always a way of "doing this or that," the worst scenario of thought.

The consequences related to fear based on threats include:

- "I would be careful/would take care if it were me."

- "If you do not listen to me, you will regret it."

- "Test and see what happens."

- "You will not like the consequences."

During the US presidential election in 2016, Hillary Clinton and Donald Trump tried to manipulate the public to vote for them:

"Imagine it in the Oval Office in the face of a real crisis. Imagine that you submerge us in war because someone has fallen under your very thin skin. The idea of Donald Trump with nuclear weapons scares me to death. That should scare everyone. " Hillary Clinton

"Radical Islamic terrorists are gaining momentum, Christians are massively executed in the Middle East, illegal immigrants are hiding in the shadows, gangs with impunity are operating in our cities, and the rate of homicides in the United States is the highest in recent years. Drugs pour across the border, bad people with bad intentions flood our airports, and you will have many world trade centers if you do not solve these problems. They want our buildings to collapse and they want our cities to be destroyed. " Donald Trump

The best way to overcome the spread of fear is to see it as it is.

If someone tries to scare you personally or sows the seeds of fear in your mind, you can ask them directly, "Are you trying to scare me?"

Weakness

Whatever your weakness is:

- greed
- lust
- money
- power
- pride
- sex
- fear

Some people deliberately try to use them against you to manipulate you.

If they know that you are suffering from anxiety, they will constantly try to fear you more. If they know that you have a strong ego, they will constantly tell you how good you are.

Advertisers love this strategy and use it to manipulate people constantly. They know that most people are sheep and blindly copy everything celebrities tell them, so they hire celebrities to promote and sell their products. They also know that there are many people with a big ego, so they produce ads that appeal to the ego and set a false trap to change you and make you better than others. Men can become "winners," and women can become "goddesses."

Peer Pressure

Some people will do something and convince you that everyone else is doing it (as if following the crowd):

- "Come on. We're all waiting for you. You're delaying everyone else!"

- "You're the only one who thinks that!"

Advertisers and the media often use a subtle form of peer pressure, known as "social proof," as they are aware that a lot of people like following famous people and will blindly follow celebrities and their styles, no matter how ridiculous they are. That's why most ads show pictures of others (especially celebrities and good-looking men and women), using the product to convince them that everyone else does, and you should too.

Sex

Sex is sold and used by advertisers around the world to manipulate people (especially men) to buy their products and services. About 25% of ads contain some form of sexual image.

Sex is also used to make popular music videos. Let's be honest, most of the music videos these days seem to be selling sex more than music.

Sex can also be used as a weapon, and often is, with men and women flirting to get what they want. Sex can be a motivator and a great tool for manipulation.

Illusion of Choice

A favorite trick used by parents, teachers, managers, and providers is to offer you several options that lead to the same result. No matter what you choose, they will win, and you will lose. It's like throwing a coin and saying, "My heads wins, your tails loses."

For example:

- "Go now or later?"

- "Start now or later?"

- "Do you want a 6-month plan or to pay everything now?"

Lying

If there is something in common among all manipulators, then it is lying.

The manipulators, without hesitation, will lie and/or cheat to get what they want.

Why do people lie? To:

- avoid embarrassment and save face

- avoid punishment

- not take responsibility

- avoid having to provide a service to someone

- not hurt the feelings of others

- get what they want

- get out of something that they don't want to do

- sound impressive or important

- cheat/manipulate

- influence/convince

Manipulators not only love to lie but they exaggerate. Some people exaggerate their achievements in trying to impress and manipulate, while others may try to manipulate by exaggerating their problems and difficulties, trying to gather sympathy and money.

"There is only one way... to get anybody to do anything. And that is by making the other person want to do it. " Dale Carnegie

People do what they want, not what you want them to do. But, if you can convince people

that an idea is theirs, they are much more likely to agree with it because they will still feel control over the decision-making process and will not feel manipulated.

How do you convince others that their idea is yours? Incorporate ideas and suggestions into their mind and then allow them to come to your conclusions as if it was their idea from the beginning. For example, McDonald's everywhere offers posters that asks you a question: "Hungry?"

Your partner may try to sow the seed in your mind, asking, "Do you think we should go on vacation soon? I heard that Hawaii is good at this time of the year... "

Control

Probably the most powerful and least understandable manipulation weapon is frame control.

What does frame control mean? It's all about making someone else fit into your idea of reality, and then encouraging them to see things from your perspective.

In an interview, an employer might set the frame as:

"Let's see if you're good enough and you have what it takes to work here."

If you were the interviewee, you would like to change this framework to:

"You are interested in me, or you wouldn't waste time interviewing me. What will you say or do to convince me to come and work for you?"

As a general rule, the person who is the most dominant is the one who controls the structure, which is the tacit value of the interaction:

- When a child talks to a father, the father controls the frame.
- When a student talks to a teacher, the teacher controls the framework.

- When an employee talks to a boss, the boss controls the framework.

- In friendship or relationship, as a rule, who cares less or has the most tangible value controls the structure.

Now that you understand what framework management is, pay attention to the following frameworks, which manipulators will often try to establish on you:

- They are the adult, and you are the child.

- They are "big brother," and you are "younger brother."

- They are the leader, and you are the follower.

- They are the teacher, and you are the student.

- They are better than you, and you should try to impress them.

- Their opinions, beliefs, and perspectives are more reasonable than yours.

- Their wishes and goals are more significant than yours.

- Their time is more precious than yours.

- You owe them and, in some way, they are entitled to something from you.

If you buy into any of these frames, you have already lost.

A manipulator will try to control the frame and force you to enter your reality, no matter how ruined and distorted. They will never allow themselves to enter your reality, nor will they allow themselves to see things from your point of view unless it is to gather information they can use against you.

If you want someone to play to your tune, then control that frame and fit it into your reality. But, if you do not want another person to manipulate you, you cannot allow them to control the frame, and you must refuse to play their manipulative, intellectual games.

CHAPTER FIVE

Techniques of Emotional Manipulation

What is Emotional Manipulation?

Let me ask you a simple question—how would you feel if you realized that all along you have been acting out a script someone else has written for you? In simpler words, what would you feel like if you realized that you have not been in charge of your actions all this time? It certainly feels scary, as well as annoying. This is exactly what emotional manipulation is all about. Most people tend to use the phrase emotional manipulation in regular parlance, but not a lot people know what they are talking about. So, it's time to set the record straight.

Emotional manipulation can be social as well as psychological, and the person using it does so to influence your behavior or response to a situation in a manner that suits their needs. It is quite right to call it manipulation because you are merely acting out someone else's script while thinking that you are true to yourself. The approach to emotional manipulation isn't usually forceful, but it has more to do with preying on your emotions—or mind— to exploit you to suit their purpose.

It is hard to see anything good in manipulation. Manipulators use what belongs to someone else in a covert way to fuel their desires, without asking for the other's permission. The issue isn't with the secrecy; usually, manipulators tend to make others do things that they normally might not do and might have even objected to.

Why Understand about Emotional Manipulation Tactics?

If you aren't aware of the different methods or tactics that manipulators usually use on you, then you will never be able to break free of their hold on you. You will continue to deceive yourself into a false sense of security—that you are in control of your life when you actually aren't. Once you are aware of the common methods of manipulation, then you can identify them when someone tries to use them on you. Emotional manipulation is certainly not a desirable thing, but there might be times when you will need to apply them to attain what you want from those who refuse to cooperate with you, at least initially.

Essentially, an emotional manipulator tends to work with the weak points in the psychology of their victims. Manipulators continuously try to look for a weak point in their victim's psyche that they can use to their advantage.

A primary characteristic trait that all emotional manipulators exhibit is secrecy. They always tend to work behind your back to achieve their goals, although they might start to blatantly exhibit their bravado once they have a firm grip on you. Manipulators tend to be great listeners naturally, and that's one of the reasons why they succeed— they pay great attention to all the details that you reveal to them in discussions, and they try to pick on those details and use them to their advantage.

Deception is an unalienable trait of a manipulator. When you think about it, that's all they do—deceive others. Armed with their cunningness, a manipulator can make you perceive something as black when it is in fact, white. If you think you have never been manipulated in your life, then you need to think again, or maybe you haven't come across a great manipulator until now. If you have been manipulated in the past, then you will notice that their personality was always domineering—at times this is obvious.

Emotional Manipulation Tactics

In this section, you will learn about the different emotional tactics that manipulators use on others. These tactics aren't just limited to the ones that are discussed in this section; however, if you want to avoid being manipulated in your life and you want to live your life on your terms, then you need to learn to recognize these common tactics.

Projection

Projection is one of the most prominent tactics that manipulators use.

Essentially, it is a diversionary tactic that emotional and psychological manipulators use to project all their deficiencies, as well as shortcomings, onto another person. Instead of stepping up and taking responsibility for their actions, they try to make someone else the fall guy and take the blame for it all. Manipulators project their faults onto someone unsuspecting. It is a tactic of psychological abuse that essentially transfers the burden of guilt from them to someone else. They are trying to paint a clear picture of themselves by making someone else look rather unfortunate. In any lousy situation, the manipulator often skirts free of all blame.

You might have come across people who behave in this manner in your life. As soon as a problem is identified or a defect is found, they conveniently transfer it all onto their victim. For instance, think of a lazy employee who hasn't been doing well at work and as such, the firm he works for has found it difficult to break even. Since this person is an emotional manipulator, they will conveniently blame it all on the leaders of the firm. You will notice that the manipulator will label the authority figures in the organization as being incompetent and ineffective while completely forgetting about their unproductive work and laziness that contributed to the financial woes.

You might also have such a person as a partner in your relationship. Instead of simply coming clean about their need for some intimacy, they will try to make you feel like you are the one that's being clingy, and by obliging you, they are doing you a favor. They try to make you look weaker to make themselves appear stronger. If you take a moment and think about it, you will notice that they are the ones who are weak.

Look out for people who are always noticing the faults in others constantly. Such people are merely projecting their shortcomings onto others around them.

Gaslighting

What does gaslighting mean? It's when you cause someone to doubt themselves about whether something is real or not.

This technique is frequently used by emotional and psychological manipulators. They do this in a subtle manner that will make you question your beliefs, and even make you think twice about all those things that are sacred to you.

For instance, let us assume that you've just graduated from college and received the trophy for showcasing great academic skills. In such a situation, an emotional manipulator will try to make you feel like such a thing didn't happen, or they will act in such a manner that you will feel unworthy of your achievement. Also, an emotional manipulator might make such statements that will make you feel like you aren't capable of achieving the feat that you did.

Now let's consider another situation where you are suspecting that your partner is using you or cheating on you. If the partner is a manipulator, then their go-to tactic will be to put such questions forward that will make you feel like all your doubts are nothing more than a figment of your imagination and aren't real. This is, perhaps, the most common reason why a lot of people stay trapped in an unhealthy relationship, in spite of seeing red flags all around them.

Denial

It can be quite difficult to distinguish between lying, denial, and the distortion of facts in any form of emotional manipulation. A manipulator doesn't necessarily have to be opposed to the truth, but their "alleged" acceptance of it is only to serve the ulterior motive of manipulating you later.

Denial is something that all emotional manipulators use—they might agree with something only to deny it later.

This behavior is not an accident.

From the get-go, they know that there will come a time when an issue will challenge their competence, and they are, therefore, prepared to deny that such an argument even took place!

For instance, a person might be asked to fill in for the position of a secretary at a company and could agree to it initially, but as soon as the demands of work start flowing in, he might deny that he ever even agreed to fill in for the post in the first place.

The same type of behavior can be exhibited in a relationship—the manipulator might not define the relationship and might make the victim assume something that they know they didn't agree to. So, as soon as the problems start to creep in, the manipulator will deny ever being in a relationship and will instead start to blame the victim.

Being in a relationship with an emotional manipulator is very unhealthy. They are the ones who make all the rules and change them to suit their needs, and it ends up leaving the victim feeling quite confused. When someone manipulates you emotionally, you might start to question yourself and even accept blame, regardless of whether you are at fault or not.

Intimidation

If an emotional manipulator perceives you to be a threat, then they often resort to intimidation to silence you. Part of this tactic is to stay close to you and talk to you in a manner that's a combination of aggressiveness and subtlety. They tend to look you in the eyes and have a strange body language so that you lose your train of thought in their hopes you stop arguing with them. They often use this tactic once they realize that it is easy to frighten or cajole you.

Don't forget that it is a basic trait of all manipulators to try and identify your weak points so that they can't use them against you. If a manipulator realizes that you get scared easily, then they will capitalize on this fear by using intimidation and threats. A way to fix this situation is by overcoming your fears and standing up for yourself. There is a simple way in which you can prevent this from happening. If you have just met someone or you don't fully trust an individual yet, then it is a good idea to keep your fears, insecurities or weaknesses to yourself. If you reveal too much, too soon, then be aware that they can use it against you. You can ask for help as and when you need it, but don't let the manipulator feel that you are scared of anything—including them.

Magnify Their Problems

It is a part of a manipulator's tactics to magnify their problems and diminish yours. This is usually done subtly, and you will not even realize it when they do it.

Manipulators tend to pretend that they sympathize with you and what you are going through and might even express some empathy, but this is only temporary, and it shields their intentions. However, you will soon notice that they keep bringing up their problems and start magnifying their troubles to make yours seem insignificant.

A manipulator will always bring up their problems as soon as you mention yours. Instead of helping you find a solution to your problems, they will bring up their allegedly bigger troubles to diminish the intensity of yours. This will, effectively, end any discussion that you were having about your problems. This unfair comparison tends to be quite annoying and frustrating since it doesn't give you the sympathy that you are looking for, and it will make you feel foolish for even bringing up your problems in the first place. They will make you feel like you are intolerant or that you don't have the willpower to deal with your problems, and will make you feel bad about even thinking about your troubles when theirs are "much worse."

Intellectual Bullying

Another tactic that emotional manipulators use is intellectual bullying. They try to manipulate you by bombarding you with intellectual facts that can overwhelm you easily. Now, don't get me wrong—the manipulator might not quote accurate facts, but they are aware of the fact that you don't have the necessary access or the opportunity to verify and validate their claims. They try to portray themselves as an authority that you cannot dispute, allowing them to get their way with you.

This form of emotional manipulation is often used in financial institutions and while making sales. You don't have the opportunity to validate their alleged facts or claims, and since they are often sweet-talkers, you will easily fall prey to their tactics without being aware of it. The only way to avoid this is by ensuring that you are well-informed before deciding. It doesn't mean that you must know everything about everything; it simply means that you need to have an idea of what they are talking about.

Intentional Digression

Digression is a tactic where the manipulator deviates from the usual course of discussion and moves onto a topic that is completely unrelated to the subject at hand. Manipulators play this card when they realize that you are holding them accountable for a certain act or deed of theirs. For instance, if you ask someone why the floor is a mess and it hasn't been cleaned yet and they promptly remind you of the UEFA

Champions League match from the other day. Of course, the person realizes that football is your weakness and the only way to distract you from the issue at hand is by diverting the topic to something else that you enjoy.

Name-Calling

A common trait of an emotional manipulator is that they always have a rather exalted but often false opinion of themselves. They believe that they are correct and others are wrong, always.

Most people who resort to any form of emotional manipulation tend to be narcissists. So, if you bring up a topic that challenges their ego by questioning their thoughts or opinions, then you must be prepared to get called more names than the one that's given to you at birth. Truth be told, if you aren't thick-skinned and are at all sensitive to criticism, then you will easily succumb to their manipulative tactics, even if it is out of sheer frustration. Being called a fanatic, a fascist, an extremist, a troublemaker or even an idiot, along with other choice adjectives, can make anyone feel annoyed, and even dejected. Once you feel any such negative emotion, you make it quite easy for the manipulator to prey on that vulnerability and make you feel bad about yourself.

So, every time you challenge a manipulator, be prepared for them to dirty your intentions to silence you.

Conditioning

Conditioning is a psychological technique used to train an animal or a human being towards a specific trait or taste that the trainer wants to inculcate in them. Of course, this would be done covertly and subtly so that the victim doesn't get suspicious—the victim wouldn't even realize that the manipulator is selling the idea to them and cornering them.

When it comes to emotional manipulation, the manipulator will think of the victim as a "pet project" that needs to be trained, and that they are the trainer. This is essentially a technique that will help them get rid of the victim's initial thoughts, encouraging them to embrace the manipulator's desires.

For instance, if you think that you are someone who values honesty, then the emotional manipulator will show you everything that you stand to gain, but only if you are dishonest. In this manner, the manipulator will slowly start to condition you to associate success with negative and undesirable values.

Gossiping and Stalking

The primary aim of any manipulator is to gain absolute control over you. However, when it seems like you are difficult to control or that it isn't going according to the manipulator's plan, then the manipulator will quickly change their tactics to control how others see you.

They try to change others' opinions of you by spreading vile and vicious rumors about you behind your back. In some cases, they might even start stalking you.

Manipulators may also try to intimidate you and try to create a negative image about you. For instance, let us assume that you are dating someone who uses this tactic.

When you drop any hints about breaking up with her or ending the relationship due to her habits, she'll go around gossiping and spreading vile rumors about you. The point is that manipulators will prevent others from getting to know your version of facts, and will start creating a story that inspires general dislike toward you.

Let me continue the example mentioned above and take it one step further. If your partner starts spreading a rumor amongst your circles of friends that you have been cheating on them, and that that's the reason why the relationship has come to an end, it will quickly turn the tables on you, even when you aren't at fault and it was nothing more than a rumor.

Love Smothering

Emotional manipulators tend to bombard their victims with a lot of love. Their sugar-coated words and behavior can easily tempt anyone into thinking that they are a perfect match and that you are hopelessly in love with them. You need to pay close attention to the things they say about their ex and see how they tend to portray such people before you as being worthless. Remember, if you are dealing with a manipulator then sooner or later, you will be subjected to the same treatment as their ex is/was. As a rule of thumb, you need to stay away from all those who degrade their exes to make you seem good. A relationship involves two people, and if it does come to an end, then both parties are responsible, not just one.

An honest person will never try to ride on their past to make their present seem great. Bringing down a person before you so that you sympathize with them is a technique of emotional manipulation. By trying to earn your sympathy, they try to manipulate you. They can quickly smother you with love so that you turn a blind eye toward everything else that they do.

Bad Surprises

Surprises are exciting, especially when they are pleasant ones and are from our favorite people. However, a manipulator might use a surprise to throw you off your game. Or, they promise that they will do something and then not keep up their promise in the last moment.

The tactic that's used here is to get a psychological advantage over the victim by placing them in such a situation where they cannot do anything other than concede to their demands.

Ultimately, when the victim has no other option, the manipulator will present an egotistical demand, leaving the victim feeling stranded and with only one way to go—the manipulator's way. They usually wouldn't have any idea of the surprise, and it will be presented in such a sneaky manner that it will make the victim feel like the other person is dependable.

Backing out on a promise is quite malicious, and it can cause a lot of harm to someone who is depending on that promise being met.

For instance, if you are in desperate need of some money and a person has promised to help you out, but in the eleventh hour that person presents a rather irrational demand that you need to fulfill before receiving the monetary assistance that was promised to you, then you have no other choice but to concede to that demand.

Personality Marketing

In this tactic, someone tries to sell their allegedly good traits to you even before you have a chance to get to know them properly. This will come up in a secretive manner, upselling their qualities and marketing something good about themselves to you when they sense that you are looking for a specific trait.

For instance, let us assume that you are looking for a partner who swims well. An emotional manipulator in such a situation will present themselves to be an excellent swimmer to win over your affection, exploit you, and probably dump you once they've had their share of fun.

When a person tries to pretend to be good at something to win you over, be very wary. Once they manage to get their hands on you and get what they want, only then will they reveal their true colors.

Demeaning Sarcasm

It might seem like they are joking, but manipulators do it subtly and sneakily, by mentioning things you are struggling with so that they can trigger your insecurities and overpower you. They usually employ this technique when they notice that you are getting attention or recognition that they believe is greater than theirs.

Can you imagine someone making jokes about a failed marriage or a rather discouraging exam in public? Of course, these things are anything but funny, but the way a manipulator does it will make you feel like they are goofing around. Their true intention is to make your immediate audience realize that you are far from being perfect or that you are not as worthy as they seem to think you are.

Manipulators tend to masquerade their intentions of hurting you in the form of demeaning sarcasm. On the face of it, it might seem like they are clowning around, but they intend to make you feel bad about yourself or make you question your self-worth. There is nothing wrong when a group of friends is cracking jokes at someone else's expense, as long as they don't harm that person in any manner—mentally or emotionally.

Triangulation

If you have a partner who is emotionally or psychologically manipulative, then you will be familiar with this tactic. It is one of the primary traits of an emotional narcissist.

This tactic aims to validate their wrongdoings or foul acts toward you by making you doubt the third party. They might be mentally abusive to you, and when you react by letting them know that such behavior isn't acceptable, they will conveniently direct your attention to someone else. They aim to make you feel like you are overreacting even when you aren't.

For instance, if your partner was physically abusive to you and you protest about it, then the manipulator will conveniently point out that one of your friends' husbands slapped her and she didn't say a word. By doing this, they are not only distracting you but are also trying to make you feel like you are overreacting. Also, the manipulator is trying hard to validate the abuse dished out.

Triangulation is a defining characteristic of an emotional manipulator.

Boundary Testing

A manipulator will never trespass your boundaries in one go. Instead, they do something that's known as "boundary testing" to see how far they can push you and your limits.

It is quite obvious that when one boundary is crossed without any retaliation whatsoever, then it will lead to another boundary being crossed; this repeats until they are firmly settled in your head. This is how a lot of abusers start their mindless acts.

They might talk to you in a condescending manner, and you might display behavior that's considered to be excessively understanding. For instance, if your partner breaks dishes in a drunken rage, you might write it off as a single incident, and that it is a one-time thing and aren't too hard on her. If you do this, you give the partner a chance to do the same thing again.

The reason why this situation escalates is you show them empathy whenever they trespass, instead of standing up to them and putting your foot down.

For a chronic manipulator, this is a green signal to push you a little harder and further the next time.

Judging

This is a tactic that is never hidden. A manipulator does this in plain sight where anyone can see it. They will try to pick on you deliberately, and you will be able to discern for yourself that it was intentional. There is nothing you can do while you are being judged unfairly by them.

This habit of being judgmental of others is a predominant characteristic of all emotional manipulators. They will keep reminding you of your faults by constantly bringing them up and by ignoring all the good that you are trying to do. So, an emotional manipulator will portray you in such a way that everyone can see all your faults but not the good—if everyone thinks that you are nothing but trouble, it gives the manipulator's ego quite a boost. So, by constantly judging you and by making you feel bad about yourself, they are trying to make themselves seem better.

Silent Treatment

How does it feel when your partner refuses to talk to you while you are in the middle of a discussion? Chances are quite high that you will start to wonder if you are doing something wrong and will start to blame yourself for the way you were probably discussing things.

For instance, let us assume that you and your partner are discussing splitting up the EMI payments equally so that it is easier for you both. Midway through the discussion, your partner goes silent, and you are left to wonder what you said that was wrong. And so, the next time you need to discuss any monetary matters with them, you will think twice, and might not even bring it up due to the fear of upsetting them.

Feigned Ignorance

In a bid to evade any responsibility, manipulators will make you feel like they don't have the knowledge or the skills to carry out the task that you asked them to do. Not only will they feign ignorance, but they will also make you feel like your skillset is superior to theirs, and try to play on your ego to make you do their work. This is often used by employees in an organization.

You will learn more about this tactic and the different ways in which you can spot whether you are being manipulated—including tips to overcome manipulation—in the coming chapters.

CHAPTER SIX

Psychological Manipulation in the Workplace

In an ideal world, you will dance your way working with happy colleagues, and even the bad ones will be good enough to let themselves be seen with ominous and frightening makeup and attire (figuratively, not literally).

Unfortunately, the real world has nothing to do with this. You can be the same delightful worker, surrounded by songbirds and bright flowers directly from a Disney movie, but the guys you need to watch out for will not wear a funny suit surrounded by minions shouting, "Hail Mogambo!" (a Despicable Me reference, for those of you who didn't pick that up!)

Amongst your pleasant circle of friends, there may be people who will compliment you, support you, and even laugh along with you, all the while using this time to secretly dig a big hole for you to step into "accidentally."

What makes people like this dangerous is their innate ability to manipulate a situation such that you end up looking bad and they shine—like a freshly sharpened knife waiting to stab someone. If you spend sufficient time with them, then you will start to feel like a worthless bum. These people are adept at controlling their emotions and only projecting what they want to be seen to the world. They never reveal their true intentions, and before you know it, they will ensnare you.

Here are some phrasing examples of psychological manipulations that your work colleagues might use on you:

- strengthen your confidence

- you're like the most brilliant guy I've seen

- I'll make you my favorite pet!

The narcissistic manipulator must feed the attention of everyone around them. Therefore, whenever you meet someone for the first time and immediately notice that you are going out of your way to charm your new friend, be careful! These people often start by giving you all the compliments in the book to get you hooked onto them. Once this is done, they start to play you like a violin.

Although it might feel quite sensational and your ego might be stoked, it is always better to keep your feet firmly planted on the ground. A couple of tempting words can be the perfect snare that a manipulator can use to make you take up their share of work and work on that massive assignment that they have been putting on hold. It will be a long and torturous route with little or no gain. So, be wary of such individuals.

Shaking your reality

How often did you notice something negative that a friend/colleague/family member from hell did, with the sole intention of making fun of you? The classic narcissist/manipulator/psychopath/sociopath focuses on changing your idea of reality and making it feel like it is a figment of your imagination, and whatever happened, didn't. Apart from this, all this will make you feel like you are slowly losing your mind.

Give in to them for long enough and, little by little, you will begin to doubt everything, as if it is some alternate reality that your imagination has sprouted.

Projection of Flaws

"Did you ever wonder why I'm behaving badly?"

Phrases such as this one are known as projection. A narcissistic manipulator ensures that their defects are nothing but a mere projection of your flaws on them. In a sense, these tactics are particularly useful when a manipulator has to explain their wrongdoing, and they do so by simply shifting responsibility onto your blameless shoulders.

It is quite similar to what you might hear from a cheating partner. "I am not cheating. It's all in your head. It is you being clingy and it is ruining a perfectly good relationship that we have. Your imagination is running wild," and so on and so forth.

Or, the head of the government could say that they could govern the country better if it were not for the reluctance of the people who keep questioning him every step of the way.

In contrast to physical abuse, there is a change of guilt or a projection. Such people at work tend to hide their inefficiencies or unproductiveness and find a way to blame others for their shortcomings:

"If you gave me a better project, I would do a better job. You are not a good manager."

Digression to Win Arguments

A popular technique of manipulation is to direct an argument or conversation to a completely different tangent, especially by asking something sensitive. The idea is to obscure or bother the victim, which comes from a very insecure place in their minds.

They do this because they seem to think of the victim as a threat to their perceived grandeur. Traditionally, politicians tend to use this technique to rile up masses against any opposition that they face.

A manipulator can go to the extent of saying something as incredulous as, "So, you don't agree with the existing decision-making policy? Then you must not love the country." Or, "You are sexist if you find some flaw with the way in which she manages this project."

Belittling Your Opinion

"Your opinion does not matter. You are driven by your emotions and aren't practical."

In a rather feeble attempt to insult their opinion, a manipulator will resort to labeling the victim as something bad, to prevent themselves from thinking too hard. With the increasing popularity of social networks in today's world, we can now see all the bullies coming out of their hiding places and reaching for their intended targets.

Most of the statements that these people make are baseless and irrational. They are merely trying to belittle opinions in a bid to make themselves seem superior. If not, they are doing so to make others feel like they aren't cut out for the job.

Extreme Labeling

"Not only do you think I'm wrong, but you're also convinced that I'm never right."

Manipulators often make extreme and absurd statements to show everyone how partial the victim is. What's their motive? To highlight the victim's injustice.

Let's say a colleague makes rude jokes about how you dress. If you call them out on it, and if they turn out to be a narcissist, a counterattack will definitely be declared.

"Are you really that sensitive?" or, "You need to grow thick skin" are the usual responses from manipulators.

Never Appreciate

"So, you think that you can dance? Can you dance while solving a complicated equation?"

Nothing you ever do will ever be satisfactory for a manipulator. If it is satisfactory, then you are no longer the punching bag for the manipulator. And, without you to feed their giant and bloated ego, they will have to go through the cumbersome process of finding another human punching bag to serve their purpose.

Here are some typical manipulator responses to consistently put a victim down:

Is it hard to be single at this age?

Oops, when did you get married?

You've been married for so long, and you still don't have any kids?

Oh, you do? Well, they are teenagers now? Nice!

Does it bother you that these are young people who will soon need to get married and live with their own children?

Cruel Jokes and Offensive Sarcasm

"Did you skip sleep last night to work on this presentation? I wish you'd informed me about it or I wouldn't have wasted 20 minutes in the morning to complete it."

Toxic people like to abandon their victims, make cruel jokes or use sarcasm when the victims don't suspect it. The idea here is to look smarter while you look like a failure.

Devalue your Achievements

"That's a great plan, and everyone seems to be talking about it; however, are you sure that you want to show this to the manager? Don't you think you should reconsider it?"

Manipulators tend to act slowly, and they try to take some time to earn the trust of their victim. In fact, it is quite similar to the way in which a snake plays with its prey before eating it. Once they earn the victim's trust, then the victim is nothing more than putty in their hands.

Hunt and then play the victim

"I don't know why he's annoyed; I just asked where the monthly report is."

(Thirty times since the manipulator called the victim at 4 a.m.!)

Manipulators can play intellectual games that are often too complicated for an average person's intellect. They provoke their victims with unbelievable shots and comments and then use their natural antagonistic reactions to prove that their victims are the irrational ones.

In a workplace, where impressions are important, the victim's reactive aggression will be perceived negatively.

Push you to Your Limits

"I am sorry that I called you a fool the other day at work; however, it isn't my fault that the presentations you create are worse than the ones that a kid in middle school can do."

If you feel like you have overcome the manipulator's attempts to humiliate you, beware of even stronger attempts. Manipulators love being able to push your limits until you reach your breaking point. They love to trouble and torture their victims (emotionally and mentally).

Veiled Threats

"Why did you even think that you could send this report directly to the manager? I did tell you to check with me before you send it, didn't I? How dare you!"

This is the final tool for manipulation in a manipulator's arsenal. They are usually smart enough to disguise their ways; however, if you are someone who is not as open to manipulation, they feel that their control is under threat. They then switch to more natural responses, such as threats and name-calling.

CHAPTER SEVEN

Recognize Emotional Manipulation in Relationships

Detect Manipulation

The cornerstones of any healthy relationship are mutual trust, respect, and security. Even if one of these elements is missing, the entire relationship could come crashing down.

Each partner needs to feel like they are valued and loved unconditionally, without any strings attached. They need to feel like they are being accepted for who they are and that they don't have to change to please their partner. Relationships are about accepting and loving each other in spite of flaws and vulnerabilities. This is the idyllic basis for a good relationship, but, of course, at times we all lack this ideal.

It's common to use passive-aggressive techniques to display our pain or to get our way in a disagreement. We can tell lies or hurl words at each other to protect ourselves and face our own anguish.

Many of us can be a little egocentric, but emotionally sound and healthy people tend to be aware of their behavior and can rectify it, apologize, and start again by adopting a healing and gentle approach to resolve conflicts and come to agreeable terms.

This mutual respect, trust, and security are essential in all relationships, regardless of whether it is a marriage or a relationship with family or friends.

Both partners need to commit themselves to a healthy relationship and have the necessary emotional intelligence so that their relationship flourishes.

What is emotional manipulation?

Emotional manipulators tend to use certain behaviors and words to get their way and encourage the victim to do something that is favorable to them.

Emotional manipulations are quite sneaky and subtle and will often leave the victim feeling rather confused and unbalanced. It can also be obvious and demanding where different negative emotions like fear, shame, and guilt are used to stun the victim.

In any case, emotional manipulation is unacceptable, and the more it is allowed to continue, the more strength and confidence the manipulator acquires in the toxic relationship. If it continues, then all the remnants of a healthy relationship are successfully destroyed and all that's left are emotional scars.

Here are the different signs of emotional manipulation in a relationship. As soon as you notice these signs, have a conversation with your partner about the same. If the partner doesn't change their ways, then it could be a good time to remove yourself from the relationship.

Turning your Words Against You

A manipulator usually has difficulty accepting any responsibility for their acts or deeds and will often find a way to turn them around and shift the blame onto you so that they don't feel any remorse. Instead of feeling bad for their behavior, they conveniently shift all the blame to their partner and walk away without any guilt whatsoever.

For instance, you might have a genuine complaint that your partner doesn't help around the house. Instead of being apologetic for their lack of participation, acknowledging their faults, and mending their ways, a manipulator will instead retort with, "You wouldn't ask me to help around the house if you were aware of all the stress that I am under?"

Or, they might even offer a quasi-apology like, "I am sorry that I was working all night long and am in no position to help you now. I know I should have probably told you about all the stress that I am under, but I figured that you understood how stressed I am. I think I am coming down with the flu or something."

This type of manipulation is, in fact, worse than no apology. This form of a quasi-apology does only one thing—guilt trip the partner and make them feel like they are unreasonable, when, in fact, all that the partner is expecting is something that the other partner had initially promised.

Your response to such emotional manipulation:

If the apology doesn't seem to be genuine, or if the other person answers with a defensive jab or starts to guilt trip you, then you must not let them get away with it. If you allow them to get away with it once, they will make a habit of doing it again. Make it quite clear that you need an unconditional apology and that their behavior isn't acceptable and must be changed immediately.

Saying Something and Denying It

A manipulator might say, "Yes" to the request or as a commitment to you, and then, when it's time to keep up their word, they will easily forget that they have ever agreed in the first place.

An experienced manipulator may distort any prior conversation or reproduce it according to their needs to evade responsibility and to also make you feel like it is your fault and that you are being demanding or even ridiculous.

Emotional manipulation causes you to doubt yourself and feel bad or guilty for challenging the manipulative partner.

Your response to such emotional manipulation:

If you are experiencing anything of this nature, then it is time to turn the tables on the manipulator. You need to employ their tactics against them. If the manipulator blames things on your "poor memory," then ensure that you make a note of the promises that your partner makes.

Record the details and date, send it to yourself and someone else via email. This can make the emotional manipulator angry and may cast doubt on their trust or faith in them, but in the future, it will be easy to prove your point.

Emotional Manipulators Use Guilt to Control You

This is a defining characteristic of a manipulator's behavior. The manipulator will sniff out your weaknesses, or your Achilles' heel, and will keep pushing them until you surrender, or you are cornered.

"You go to the movies without me; it's all right, I'll stay at home and finish the chores here."

"Why do your needs always come before mine? If you knew about my childhood, you would have never even asked me to do it."

"If you really want to go on a holiday with your friends, go ahead. I do not understand how you can even think about leaving the kids alone at home."

"I know we cannot afford a new car right now. It looks like I am stuck with this piece of junk. I don't think I deserve anything good in life."

An emotional manipulator knows how to play the role of the sacrificing partner, or that of a victim, quite well.

Your response to such emotional manipulation:

Do not think that you are going crazy, don't fall prisoner to them, and don't feel guilty, because their reaction is NOT your fault. Learn to resist giving into their passive pleas or requests for sympathy.

Diminish your Problems and Difficulties

Manipulators do not worry much about their important problems unless they can use them as a means to highlight their grievances.

"Do you feel irritated and sick that you had to sit in a traffic jam today?"

"Have you ever thought about how I deal with this traffic daily? It literally takes up years of my life. Be grateful that you just had to deal with this today."

"Damn it, it's terrible that you and your mother had an argument, but be grateful to have a mother; my mother is dead, and even when she was alive, we used to fight a lot more than you and your mother. I almost feel like I didn't have a mother."

A manipulator can somehow make everything about them, even when it has nothing to do with them—this shows how an emotional manipulator can turn the tables. They will do this with the intention of making you look selfish and most likely don't recognize their narcissistic behavior, nor remember a conversation about a difficulty that you are facing.

Your response to such emotional manipulation:

In such scenarios, there is little that can be done, except to leave and find someone more caring, understanding, and mature. Never expose your vulnerabilities to someone who is going to trample all over them.

Backdoor Technique

Instead of being forthcoming and direct, manipulators will avoid all forms of honest communication and, instead, will use methods that are best described as being passive-aggressive.

They might talk about you behind your back or ask someone to be their representative, so they do not have to be the stereotypical "bad guy." For instance, they might ask a friend to tell you they want to break up with you, or tell their best friend how unhappy they are in general and ask them to convey the same to you.

Your response to such emotional manipulation:

For your sake, it is a good idea to call out their behavior. Most likely, you will receive an evil and defensive reaction, but at least the manipulator understands that you are privy to what they are doing.

If this manipulative behavior happens regularly, it is time to consult counseling, or to end the relationship and move forward with your life.

Energy Drain

As they enter a room, you might sense or feel the dark aura that a manipulator carries with them. If a manipulator wants everyone in the room to notice if they are unhappy or angry in some way, then they will ensure that they are doing so. Being in a room with a manipulator, a sensitive person will most likely feel exhausted and unbalanced.

A submissive partner will quickly scamper to make the manipulator feel better by giving them the sympathy and the attention that they need.

Your response to such emotional manipulation:

If it is possible, then distance yourself from them, and I mean physically remove yourself from that room. Why must you squander your energy and good mood to accommodate the tantrums of a manipulator?

Using Aggression or Anger

Emotional manipulators usually try to intimidate others with aggressive language, hidden threats or direct anger. If they see that you feel skittish in the conflict, they will especially use it to quickly control you.

It could be that your spouse has a quick temper, and that whenever you bring up his expensive shopping sprees, he becomes angry and aggressive.

Maybe your spouse tends to raise her voice and close the door when you do something she doesn't like. They will judge your reaction to their mood and aggression and, over time, will learn how to get their own way.

Your response to such emotional manipulation:

If their anger or aggression is at a point where you feel scared or unsafe, leave immediately and call the police.

If their mood becomes out of control, they might resort to more damaging behavior (mentally, emotionally, and physically). You need to open your eyes and see them for who they are—emotional manipulators. They will stop at nothing and stoop to the lowest levels to get what they want.

Manipulators tend to look for partners who are sensitive, insecure, and gullible. They will prey on these insecurities without feeling an ounce of remorse. They will never put anyone else's needs above their own.

You can try counseling or couples' therapy to fix the situation.

Fix your Relationship

If you think your relationship is salvageable and that your partner is unknowingly manipulative, then here are a few ways in which you can fix your relationship.

Build Trust Again

An inability to trust partners can take up many different forms, such as the feeling that they are dishonest and that they are hiding something, aren't consistent and reliable. You might also feel that they aren't there when you need them and that they might take advantage of you if you seem vulnerable. These feelings will stop you from expressing your true self and can damage the relationship.

People usually initiate a relationship not for the reason that they have common values, but probably because they see something that's desirable in their partners. Over a period of time, one or both the partners might become more confident, or their needs might change. This will make them less inclined towards putting up with any differences.

Charm does wear thin when your partner doesn't help with domestic chores, and jealousy can creep in like an unwanted guest. Manipulators try to control their victims so that they feel they won't find someone better, and those who have been abused or hurt in previous relationships, or as children, will tend to have trust issues already.

A loving relationship will provide the support that people will need to explore themselves, to learn, grow, and broaden each other's horizons by bringing in their passions and interests; it will encourage spontaneity and the taking of reasonable risks; however, where there is a deficiency of trust, the opposite happens—it can make our worlds smaller and compressed, and we might try to control our partners.

When people no longer share the same fundamental values or when they can no longer trust each other, then fear, insecurity, and a sense of detachment will dominate a relationship. When this happens, you might start to push others away inadvertently, get angry for no apparent reason, and alienate yourself. When you push people away, you are pushing away the genuine love that they might have towards you.

The first thing that you will need to do is determine the reason for your trust issue; whether it was due to the way your partner behaved in the past or perhaps due to your own issues. If you aren't able to trust yourself, then you will need to see what is getting in your way. Is it your insecurity, an unresolved issue, addiction or any other reason? If the reason is something that your partner had done, then you will need to start talking about that issue with your partner in a non-accusatory manner. If necessary, think of the behaviors that aren't acceptable to you, and you can set reasonable limits to the way your partner behaves. If you are suppressing things and aspects of your personality to accommodate your partner, then you will need to address this issue as well and find common ground that will let you be yourself.

Therapy can also be really helpful in resolving trust issues.

Forego the Blame Game

This means the attribution of some bad or unfavorable outcome to our partners. This might also include that we have a better way of thinking, that we know the ways in which they have to change and trying to "fix" them according to what we think is desirable.

Whenever something goes wrong, our brain will automatically start looking for the cause and the ways in which to fix it. People might feel unsafe when they don't have control. Blaming and fixing our partners will be a means of trying to gain more control over the outcomes of important things in life.

Problems tend to be multifaceted, and most of the problems will not have a single cause. For instance, a person might be incapable of finding a job that pays well, even after trying to the best of their ability, due to geographical and economic factors, as examples. Your partner might not actually be doing anything wrong, even if it seems like he is. Also, there are some basic traits like intelligence, introversion, energy levels, and emotional sensitivity that are inbuilt and cannot be changed.

You might be viewing a particular issue through the warped lens of distortion, and your partner might have a different perspective towards the same thing. When you blame a person, their instant reaction will be to defend themselves or withdraw. This will create a negative cycle of anger, hurt, and miscommunication, none of which are desirable.

When you start blaming each other, negative communication will increase, and you might end up hurting your partner just because you want to prove that you are right. In doing this, you will be causing a lot of unnecessary damage to your relationship. Instead of trying to find out what went wrong, you and your partner might just be trying to prove the other one wrong.

You will need to take a look at the manner in which you acted, your assumptions, and how they added onto the problem. You will need to take full responsibility for your contribution to the problem; it might be simple miscommunication, unrealistic expectations, being unsupportive or getting angry. If you feel that your partner has hurt you, then you must communicate this to her in a gentle manner, instead of demanding that she behave the way you want her to.

Learn to Handle Criticisms

There are many different reasons why people will criticize their partners. They might have picked up a bad habit while growing up and might not realize the negative impact that their behavior has. At a deeper level, those who have narcissistic tendencies tend to be scared of intimacy and are vigilant for the faults in their partners because they will not want anyone to tell them that they made a wrong choice or will not want their choice to reflect badly on them. Barbed comments can also be the result of repressed anger that keeps seeping out time and time again.

Criticisms and putdowns are also used by those individuals who have abandonment issues and are untrusting; they can also erode a person's self-confidence and trust. We all have weaknesses; loving someone means that you accept and understand them for who they are, including their weaknesses and faults, and support them so that they grow in their lives. Instead of turning into a fault-finding machine, it's more helpful to be supportive—constant criticism can erode a person's character, and if you don't stop it, it can very well end a perfectly good relationship.

Start by being more compassionate and understanding. Learn to be mindful of what you are saying. Even if you are joking about something and realize that your partner isn't taking it well, it's better to stop there and then. If there is something that you don't like about your partner, instead of criticizing them about it, try and understand why they behave in that particular manner. It will help you understand your partner better.

Work on Reducing Emotional Distance

Couples can easily neglect to communicate their feelings and needs that are really important to them. Secondary emotions, like anger, are usually substituted in place of real emotions. They might also respond to their partner's attempts to ask them for change by shutting them out completely or by behaving in a passive-aggressive manner, perhaps even sidetracking an entire conversation.

No one likes to feel vulnerable, especially when they think their deepest needs and feelings will not be heard or respected by their partner. It is also likely that one partner might not know how to react or behave when the other partner expresses their unhappiness. A common response will be to try and fix the problem rather than listen empathetically. Individuals who had a traumatic childhood, suffered from abuse or loss, might get uncomfortable with their own emotions and those of others, and, as a result, fear intimacy.

Emotional distance will unnecessarily make a partner doubt whether her needs can even be fulfilled. Couples might feel more like roommates, lead separate lives, and communicate only about the errands and different logistics of maintaining a household. There will likely not be any sexual intimacy, and negative feelings of being hurt and loneliness will come to the forefront. Emotional distance can make the partners indulge in undesirable activities that can ultimately lead to the breakdown of the relationship.

If you want to start rebuilding emotional intimacy, then you will need to be your true self with your partner. You will need to be brave and willing to make certain changes to your character and might also have to give up a few habitual patterns that you might have been used to all your life.

Couples' therapy can be useful and can help in getting rid of destructive patterns. Sometimes, both partners might also need individual therapy for dealing with these issues separately. If you want to restore sexual intimacy, then both the partners will have to view it as a priority and as a means of satisfying both their urges, instead of one partner satisfying themselves at the expense of the other. This will involve restoring trust, communication, and also exploring the different ways to express intimacy.

Hurtful interactions have the power to wreck a relationship; they can cause people to shut each other out and also build a lot of unresolved anger. These are common problems that can be resolved with a little bit of effort. Every time you feel like criticizing your partner, hold back your words for a moment and think things through before saying them out loud. Words, once spoken, cannot be taken back.

If you think that it is better to end things for the sake of your happiness, then do so. You must not be trapped in a toxic relationship that slowly drains the life out of you.

CHAPTER EIGHT

Manipulative Tactics Narcissists Use

In this section, you will learn about the common tactics that a narcissist uses against their victims.

The world of a narcissist is quite complex. The disorder that they suffer from is unlike any other, and it can confuse all those around them and prevent them from understanding what is happening. But how is it that narcissists are so good at manipulating others?

Narcissists are good at manipulating others because they are always trying to look for the vulnerabilities that others have. Once they understand what is important to you, they will try to use those things against you. Some instances of vulnerabilities include any self-esteem issues or insecurities you might have about your appearance, or even the fear of being alone or losing someone close to you. Narcissists will try to find out these vulnerabilities during the love-bombing and good-listener stages of the relationship.

Narcissists try to target those who are co-dependent, i.e. someone who may have experienced a past abusive relationship or might have grown up in homes with narcissistic members of family. They may have many other problems with self-esteem and self-control, but the main reason why people stay in a relationship with a narcissist is that they do not realize the manipulator is actually a narcissist.

Ordinary people operate in what sociologists call the "just world." This fair world outlook means that we think people will treat us the way we treat them, and the world is fair, and that our morals and values are similar to those around us. This point of view is true in the vast majority of cases, except when dealing with manipulators, such as those who have narcissistic or sociopathic/antisocial personalities.

Many people believe that their partner is normal and any negative behavior they demonstrate is correctable and modifiable. Once again, we act from the perspective of the "just world," where we think that if we do something harmful or malicious, we will change it. But, in reality, narcissists and sociopaths do not care if their actions hurt others. In fact, they often get great pleasure in causing pain. In the end, the more reactions they can get from people, the more important they will feel and the more their ego will be boosted.

There is no better manipulator than a narcissist, especially if they are "hidden." A narcissist/secret sociopath will pretend (convincingly) that they have the same manners and values as the rest of society, with their ultimate goal as making sure their victim has access to everything they can wish for: Sex, attention, money, food, clothing, housing, status, etc.

But the reality is that they do not have the same morality and values that we do.

They have no morals or values at all, although they pretend that they do. They even do everything possible to show the world that they have moral values and that their values are higher than everyone else's, such as taking a position of power in their church, volunteering regularly, and verbally denouncing those who show ethically doubtful behavior.

Over time, those close to narcissists will begin to realize that they have the duality of Dr. Jekyll/Mr. Hyde in them, that their words are very different from their actions, and all the things they so strongly declare themselves against is exactly what they do. In short, narcissists are no more than emotional delinquents.

It takes some time to identify a narcissistic partner because the likelihood that our partner is an emotional manipulator is not on our radar. Therefore, when a narcissist displays any bad behavior, they are treated in the same way as another normal person who is badly behaved. The couple work through it, the narcissist is given a second chance, the couple goes to therapy, marriage programs and reads self-help books.

We know that relationships are hard work and every relationship has its ups and downs, and perhaps, in the depths of our souls, we know that there is something of value in going through the garbage to end up happy to be together after all the pain.

Many victims adhere to these beliefs for years, sometimes decades, until they get tired of riding this carousel and decide to end the relationship. The victim may experience guilt for leaving, while also feeling stupid for staying so long. (Even if you feel that this is normal, do not be so hard on yourself. You did not know you had a relationship with a person with a fixed personality disorder).

So, how can you distinguish a normal relationship from a narcissistic relationship?

Normal people in normal relationships express real regret for their misbehavior, and offer to compensate for it through consistent actions.

In a narcissistic relationship, you will notice that a narcissist will not offer any sincere apologies (if you get them!), will not have a desire to change, and if so, that only lasts while you are angry, and a narcissist will continue to sneak away and live their lives as they see fit.

In a normal relationship, the same problems (usually lies, fraud, and abuse—verbal or emotional) do not happen again and again with your partner.

Let's look at six manipulation techniques that a narcissist will often use.

Denial

As soon as you confront a narcissist about their bad behavior, they will immediately deny it like it never even happened, even if you present solid evidence. If you do manage to get the narcissist to admit anything, they will try to admit only the bare minimum and will deny all the bad bits, or admit things only to the extent that they know you are aware of.

When victims stay in a relationship with manipulative people who don't own up to their actions, they start to question their perceptions and will start to question whether the thing that they are talking about actually happened or not. Narcissists, as well as sociopaths, are such good manipulators and gaslighters that the victim is often partial toward believing their perspectives instead of trusting what they saw or experienced.

If denial doesn't do the trick for the narcissist, then they will try to combine it with all the other strategies discussed in this section.

Triangulation

Triangulation is a favorite tool for all manipulators, and is quite similar to a love triangle, except that it doesn't necessarily involve any lovers. This can happen in any relationship dynamic that involves three individuals—at work, at home or even with friends. A triangle is formed in such a way with two people, that the narcissist pits them against each other so that each thinks the other is responsible for a problem, leaving the real culprit out of the equation. As examples, a narcissist parent might turn two of their children against each other, or a narcissist husband might pit his wife against another woman.

Triangulation is brilliant in its simplicity, yet quite evil. It helps to keep the narcissist in the clear and free of all blame, frenzy, and confusion it creates, boosting the narcissist's ego—he or she gets a kick out of seeing that they are being fought over or from the knowledge that they have sufficient power to control and upset others.

Pity

Never underestimate narcissists. They always know that if they can get you to feel sorry for them, then they will be able to manipulate you in such a way that it can shift your focus from their negative behavior and instead focus on making them feel better. The narcissist might try to gain your sympathy by playing the card of a bad childhood, excessive stress at work, a terrible past relationship or even alcoholism. They might even tell the victim that they have suicidal tendencies and depression.

They can come up with rather inventive lies to distract their victim from their bad behavior. There are no limits to the lengths that a narcissist can go to achieve this goal.

Their conscience doesn't get in their way.

Guilt

"It's your fault," is the go-to line for almost all narcissists. Somehow and in some manner, the cheating, lying or any other form of bad behavior that the narcissist exhibits is all the victim's fault. They can easily make their victim feel the guilt for pointing out something that is wrong.

Perhaps your partner is telling you that you need to stay more at home, avoid going out with your friends late at night, avoid drinking or even wearing specific clothes. According to the narcissist, their behavior is always the fault of the victim. The narcissist will be quick to point out that whatever they did or said was due to your mistakes, and not theirs. An abusive partner, after a rather violent outburst, tends to blame the victim by saying that she made him act a certain way.

Narcissists are always careful with the words they use. Even when they are lying, they tend to ensure that whatever they are saying has some truth to it so that they can guilt-trip their partners.

Intimidation

They tend to make threats that are thinly veiled, or they can even come right out and threaten you.

Intimidation doesn't always have to be physical; it can even be in the form of a threat that the partner might report you for being an unfit parent, threatening to divorce you or anything like that.

A narcissist will always go to great lengths to ensure that they get what they want. Victims often stay in a relationship with a narcissist because they are too scared to leave and are worried about what the narcissist would do if they did manage to leave.

Hope

A narcissist can put on an Oscar-winning performance to get their victims to believe that all that they need is another chance to prove that they have changed. It is quite understandable why the victims tend to believe them and fall for their lies and false promises. Hope is eternal, and even if there is a sliver of hope that the narcissist might change, the victims tend to stick around.

This brings me back to the concept of a "just world": a perspective that normal people tend to have. Normal people believe that their actions, if hurtful, must be mended and that they would be sorry for their acts. Narcissists, on the other hand, will make their victims *feel* that they are sorry (it is only temporary and will not last).

Narcissists' behavior might be so outlandish that it could make the victim feel like they have hit rock-bottom. But with Narcissists, there is no rock-bottom. They are capable of making decisions based solely on their whims and fancies, and nothing else.

There is no way in which you can fix a narcissist's behavior. All that you can do is ensure that you distance yourself from such a toxic relationship.

CHAPTER NINE

Work on Self-Esteem to Overcome Manipulation

A reduced image that you have of yourself leads to low self-esteem. Self-image is your perception of yourself, the way you see yourself. Do you think you are dependable, hardworking, friendly, or an honest person? Do you feel comfortable with the way you are? Do you like what you see when you look in the mirror? Do you believe that others look and dress better than you do?

Low self-esteem thrives on several factors. For instance, do you like your job? Does your work make you happy and does it add any value to your life? Do others respect you? Low self-esteem stems from negative thinking and the criticisms that others make of you. Do you feel bogged down by the criticism you receive from others? Do you think that you lose confidence because of all this?

On the other hand, high self-esteem is precisely the opposite of everything that's been mentioned above. You will feel confident, motivated, and have a positive outlook towards life when you have a healthy self-esteem. We all tend to have a personal self-image or an opinion about ourselves; our perception of strengths, weaknesses, and beliefs are formed from an early age.

Our self-image plays a significant role in our lives, our interactions with others, and everything else that we do. Self-esteem is nothing more than the set of feelings you have about yourself. People lacking in self-esteem cannot see their worth, and they don't believe in their abilities. They tend to think that they are somehow flawed and are inferior to those around them.

It isn't always easy to figure out which category you fall under. Here are a couple of thoughts and behaviors that are usually associated with those who have low self-esteem.

Whenever someone compliments you, are you comfortable accepting it? Do you feel like you deserve the compliment, or do you say something to brush it off? Instead of brushing away compliments, you can graciously accept them. Giving is an important aspect of life, and so is receiving. When you accept a compliment willingly and graciously, you give others an opportunity to experience the happiness of giving. It shows not just your modesty but also your confidence in yourself.

Can you express your opinion freely and trust it? Whenever you have something important to say, do you take your turn and express yourself? Can you maintain eye contact with others while expressing yourself or do you always look down? Whenever you walk into a room for the first time, do you sit in the front seats? Usually, all those who opt to sit on the edge are the ones who don't want to be noticed, and this behavior is associated with those who have low self-esteem.

Are you a good judge of yourself?

Are you capable of taking negative criticism from those around you and are you capable of accepting your mistakes?

Can you work on improving yourself based on the criticism you receive, or do you get defensive or depressed?

Do you understand that a portion of the comments you receive from someone isn't representative of the general opinion that others have of you?

Can you accept your uniqueness?

You might wish to be taller, slimmer, more outgoing, and less impulsive; however, whenever you ask yourself "who am I?" do you have an answer to it that takes into consideration your uniqueness?

Even after a tiring day, can you maintain good body posture, or do you slouch?

Will you consider yourself to be optimistic or pessimistic?

Do you like wearing clothes that you want or are your choices influenced by what others think of you?

Do you do things for your satisfaction or because someone else asked you to do a particular job?

Take some time out, and answer the questions mentioned above honestly. Everyone will have faced some instance or another in their life that reduced their self-esteem. It is quite natural; however, it is essential to build it back and not let your self-esteem plummet further. Like any other personality trait, even self-esteem can be improved.

We are all born with confidence, and it is our experiences that can enhance or diminish these feelings. A child is always eager to learn more and will keep trying even after falling multiple times. So, where does this confidence disappear?

It might feel like there are plenty of barriers to self-esteem; however, if you are interested in developing yourself, then the first that you must work on is improving your self-esteem. Until you do this, it will not be easy for you to assess and achieve your goals. Low self-esteem can also prevent you from seeing what your goals are. Think of your life as an empty dartboard, and everyone around you has the potential of becoming a dart that can potentially damage your life at one point or another. Those darts are bound to hurt your self-esteem, in ways you cannot even consciously comprehend. So, what are the darts that you must be aware of and avoid? Low self-esteem provides the opening that's necessary for a manipulator. As soon as the manipulator realizes that your self-esteem is your weakness, they will try to exploit it, and you in the process.

Let us take a look at the different things that act as barriers to your self-esteem. Once you are aware of the different barriers, you can work on improving yourself.

Negative work environment: Have you ever heard the phrase, "It's a dog-eat-dog world?"

This is a belief that it feels like everyone is fighting to get ahead of each other. Beware of this, because this is where all those who aren't appreciative tend to thrive. In such a scenario, no one is going to appreciate anyone else, so stay away from such a negative environment. It will just bring you down, and it will shatter your self-esteem.

Don't get involved in power games or other negative behaviors that will make you think less of yourself. Compete with others on your terms, if you have to compete at all.

Subconscious: Our minds work consciously and subconsciously.

Our conscious mind is responsible for all the actions that require active thought. However, most of our minds work subconsciously.

Our subconscious can influence us a great deal. If you think positively about yourself, then you will feel good about yourself; however, any deep-seated feelings of inadequacy, incompetence, or anything that's negative will make you feel poorly about yourself. Your self-esteem can take a hit without realizing it.

Your thoughts create your reality, and by changing the way you think, you can recreate your reality as well.

It isn't that difficult; you need to condition your mind to think positively. Things don't necessarily always go as you planned them to happen, and you might or might not achieve everything you have set out to do. Failures and setbacks are common; however, what matters is your ability to bounce back.

Negative self-talk: We all have a tiny voice in our head that keeps telling us that we aren't good enough, that we might fail, or that we cannot achieve our goals.

It is quite normal, and everyone thinks such thoughts; however, when you start indulging in too much negative self-talk, you are setting yourself up for failure.

If you don't believe in yourself, it is highly unlikely that someone else will. Try to change this pattern and indulge in some positive self-talk. If you tell yourself that you are good at what you do and that you deserve to attain your goals, after a while, you will start to believe it.

Whenever you hear negative self-talk, stop it immediately. All such talk does is make you feel depressed and disappointed with yourself.

Making use of powerful imagery will also help you understand what you will experience and feel when you have managed to achieve your goals, which is sufficient motivation to keep on pushing.

The behavior of others: You will come across all sorts of negative people in your life, from gossipers to naggers, complainers, and backstabbers. It all depends on whether you let their negativity get to you or not. Negative behavior will damage your self-esteem and self-development. Learn to identify such behavior and avoid it.

Change: Don't resist change. Change is a natural process, and there will be stagnation without change. Go with the flow and don't stress too much about it. Think of change as an opportunity to do something better.

Past experiences: Your past must be a learning experience for you, but it must not dictate the way you behave.

If you got hurt in the past, learn from it and don't let that fear take hold of you. Each failure and mistake is a learning opportunity; treat them as such. Don't let your past experiences ruin your future for you. If you grew up hearing that you weren't good enough, how can you possibly develop positive self-esteem as an adult? If you were criticized regardless of how hard you worked and tried, it'd be more difficult to feel confident about yourself. If you don't feel comfortable in your skin, then think about the reasons that make you feel so.

It can be quite painful when the authority figures you were exposed to while growing up were disapproving. A scenario like this will make you feel dejected and unrecognized, and these feelings probably followed you into adulthood.

Negative outlook: Don't get consumed by all the negativities that exist in this world.

A negative outlook toward life will always prevent you from seeing all the good that is there in you and around you.

What is your take on self-love? More importantly, do you love yourself?

If you have any difficulty feeling, expressing, and accepting self-appreciation, then you must think about developing self-love. Self-love and self-esteem are interwoven concepts, and one cannot exist without the other.

You might have spent a lot of your time and effort demanding perfection from yourself. When you start chasing perfection, you set impossibly hard standards of success, and more often than not, you will fall short, regardless of how hard you try.

The feeling of "I'm not good enough" can stop you from making the most of the opportunities that come your way. Unknowingly, you are sabotaging your life, relationships, and career.

For instance, think of a situation where your loved one comes to you about something that's troubling him. Your friend tells you that he feels stuck and like a failure.

What will you say?

Will you react kindly to them?

You probably will, and you will try to make them feel better about themselves.

So, when it comes to you, why don't you extend the same compassion towards yourself? When you are kind to yourself and when you love yourself, your self-esteem will improve. If you don't love yourself, then don't expect anyone to ever truly love you. Self-love is the first step to finding true happiness.

Your childhood, upbringing, and several genetic traits also contribute to the way you are; however, don't ever think that your genetics determine who you are. You have the power of becoming better and of changing yourself, provided that you want to. The first steps in improving your self-esteem is understanding what self-esteem is all about and determining your level of self-esteem. By answering the questions mentioned in this chapter, and by examining and monitoring your feelings toward yourself, you should be able to decide on your level of self-confidence.

Here are some affirmations that you can use to feel better about yourself.

- I am skilled, smart, and capable.

- I have faith in myself.

- I am aware of the good qualities I possess.

- I see the best in myself and those around me.

- I am surrounded by people who bring out the best in me.

- I let go of all undesirable thoughts and feelings about myself.

- I am always growing and developing, and I love myself.

- I love my son/daughter, and I get along fine with him/her.

- I have nothing but infinite and unconditional love toward my partner.

- I respect and cherish my parents, partners, and friends.

If you are filled with positivity, then you will not need to depend on anyone else to make you feel better.

CHAPTER TEN

Psychological Manipulation Through Words

Using sarcasm as a response.

Saying that it is quite difficult to talk to you.

Speak to you as if you were a child.

Threats that are served with ultimatums. The signs of mental manipulation through communication and language are as diverse as they are tedious. These are types of emotional abuse and mental exploitation, which are quite unhealthy, and it is time that you learn to deal with them.

Licio Gelli is considered to be a sinister person in Italy's history. This agent of the so-called propaganda duo of the Masonic Lodge was a neo-fascist who specialized in manipulating the masses. This evil being once said that to control someone, you need to know how to talk and communicate effectively. He displayed that language is a weapon and can be used in a rather perverse way to dominate.

We think this to be true, though. In politics, in advertising, and this vast media universe, manipulations are almost always used to entice us, influence our choices and, ultimately, control us. Now that we are entering the private sphere, things are becoming a bit more complex.

I am specifically talking about the way we communicate with our families, co-workers and our friends. The signs of psychological, as well as emotional, manipulations are evident around us, but they are often disguised. We can also, without being aware of it, fall into the trap of using them ourselves. Therefore, it is important to know how to spot them and how to respond to them.

We must realize that it is important to not only be attentive to what we say but also of the manner in which we say it. When we approach the idea of psychological manipulation using our words, what happens initially is that it causes an imbalance in a relationship. This is the specific use of language only to benefit one person. Our naked emotions are what leads to this hidden aggression within us.

Aldous Huxley once said that words could be like x-rays. Used by the Machiavellian method, they can penetrate everything: The other's self-esteem, dignity, and even identity. So, let's learn to see how they present themselves so as to understand a little more about this damaging dynamic on a personal level. Here are nine warning signs.

Manipulating the facts

Every specialist in psychological manipulation, through words and communication, is a good strategist who is adept at distorting the truth. They will always do it to their advantage, it will reduce their share of responsibility, and they will blame others for it. Besides, they will exaggerate and hide key information and, therefore, guarantee that the balance always deviates towards their "true" version instead of the truth.

They will tell you that it is impossible to talk to you

This technique is simple, straightforward, and effective. If someone tells you that it's difficult to talk to you, then avoid exactly what they want to do. Instead, talk about the problem. They will often tell you that you are too sensitive, that you are making a mountain out of a mole hill, and that they cannot talk to you. They accuse you of what plagues them, which is poor communication skills.

Intellectual harassment

This occurs when a manipulator will bombard you with uninterrupted disputes, along with diverse information, complicated facts, and arguments to wear you down emotionally and convince you that they are right.

Ultimatums with little time for resolve

"If you do not agree with what I tell you, it's over between us."

"I'll give you until tomorrow to think about what I told you."

This kind of communication is, without a doubt, very painful and disturbing. They put you between the hammer and the anvil and will likely cause anxiety and strong, emotional suffering.

If someone respects you and loves you, then such a person will never use these "all or nothing" threats. It is nothing more than a strategy to manipulate you. The next time someone tries to do this to you, you need to do a simple thing—call his bluff. If he goes ahead with his threat (it is quite unlikely), then you will know what the relationship meant to that person.

The repetition of your name during a conversation

Whenever someone repeats your name almost constantly and melodramatically in the conversation, such an individual is using an intelligent control mechanism. By doing this, she wants to make you pay attention and to feel intimidated.

Irony and dark humor

The use of irony and dark humor, which seeks to embarrass or demean, is another common sign of psychological manipulation through words and communication. The manipulator tries to belittle you and tries to impose their "alleged" psychological superiority.

Use silence or evasiveness

"I do not want to talk about it."

"Now is not the right time."

"Why are you talking about that now?" This kind of communication is quite common among partners, especially if one of them has poor communication skills and no sense of responsibility.

Declaration of ignorance: "I don't understand what you're saying"

This is a standard tactic. Manipulators pretend they do not understand what the other person wants them to say or do, and instead play with the mind of the victim. They try to impress that the other person is complicating the situation too much and that the conversation does not make sense. This is the classic approach of a passive-aggressive manipulator, as they evade taking responsibility and seek to make others suffer.

They will let you speak first

One of the subtlest signs of mental manipulation is when one person always forces the other to speak first. With this technique, manipulators achieve several things. It helps buy time to prepare their argument, and they find your weaknesses. It is also common that, after listening to you, the emotional manipulator avoids expressing their ideas or opinions. They ask questions, and, instead of trying to reach an agreement, they seek to highlight your shortcomings.

CHAPTER ELEVEN

Silent Treatment = Emotional Abuse

The silent treatment is the refusal to participate in any oral communication with someone, often in response to a conflict in a relationship. Also known as "cold shoulder" or "obstruction," its use is a form of passive-aggressive control and in many cases can be considered a form of emotional abuse.

Sometimes in an argument there is nothing to say. The disconnection can be so clear that each party retracts into their psychological corners to think, regroup, and then resume with a mutual desire for clarity. Arguments of this kind are never pleasant, but they will come and go, perhaps leaving a new understanding after them.

Silent treatment

Considered the number one weapon in the arsenal of passive aggression, it keeps its "adversary" in a dead-end, while at the same time giving them a false sense of power. Ignoring anyone in this way can be extremely harmful and is unfair. The psychological effects can be long-lasting.

A silent situation can, usually, only be rectified when both parties are in such an absolute synchronization to avoid the phrase, "I do not need to explain why it hurts." The silent treatment involved in such a disconnect between feelings reinforces the unspoken uncertainty of the owner and, ultimately, a distrust can form that condemns the relationship.

Suffering loves company

A part of the manipulator wants to make others suffer. However, you could view the silent treatment as a form of violence—that being emotional violence. If the goal was to establish resolve and understanding, the manipulator would speak and try to balance the situation.

If you are dissatisfied with someone, then it is a good idea to talk to her about it. Human emotions can be difficult to deal with when you internalize them. So, instead of being silent with this person, ask yourself what made you so angry.

Silent treatment is almost always a tactic to avoid communication with your inner demons.

How to deal with it

If you are receiving silent treatment and wish to remain dignified, what should you do? You don't want to suffer, but you also don't want your loved one to get caught up in undesirable thoughts about your suffering.

The reaction to silent handling requires sensitivity, openness, understanding and a good dose of humility. Don't pretend that you aren't aware of the silent treatment—this will just fuel the fire. It's very tough to break the silence as the victim, because the silent treatment hurts you, yet you feel guilty—it's a muddy mixture. This combination is part of the silencer's tactics—avoid you and leave you speechless. It can be a terrible feeling.

Instinctively you want to fix something, but these cases are usually based on the fact that, in the first place, you do not know what you did wrong (in the eyes of another), or something so small that the manipulator feels the need to take control quickly.

Being at the end of such an emotional manipulation is a win-win scenario, and it takes tremendous patience to get out of this situation and be the one to break the ice, but this is what is needed for the relationship to move forward. Asking questions for clarity of the situation and expressing each other's' feelings is the trick here.

Simplicity is Key

Feeling like you have somehow slipped your loved one some poison and are now scrambling to find a suitable antidote is no way to go through life or a relationship. You don't have to accept it, you must not internalize it, and you certainly don't need to accept someone else's ploy for power, regardless of whether they are doing it consciously or unconsciously. This is a sign of failure on your part if you cannot stand up to a manipulator.

You must understand that you are not wrong and you haven't done anything that is wrong. A genuine problem is one thing, but prolonged petulance isn't.

Unless you are the sort that's overbearing, emotionally abusive or even manipulative yourself, in which case there is nothing that you and your partner must do apart from parting your ways, the sole purpose of the silent treatment is to calm you down with a couple of weary sighs.

There are two simple rules that you need to follow in your life. The first one is that you need to be kind to each other and the second is that you must be good for each other. It is not a conditional statement and is not optional. You need to ensure that these two things exist if you don't want your relationship to spin out of control.

A single word can end the silent treatment. You need to acknowledge a simple fact that you cannot read anyone else's mind and they cannot read your mind. You are not an open book, and nor are they. So, open and honest communication is necessary for all aspects of life. If there is something that needs to be addressed, then do so and don't hide behind the silent treatment. The best place to start with this is the reality, and you can take it from there.

When to use the Silent Treatment

There is a time and place for when to use the silent treatment, and in some situations it can be rather desirable; in an unhealthy relationship where one person attempts to resolve a conflict that is quickly escalating to aggression, then silence is a good way to prevent the conflict from getting out of hand. Avoid talking about the topic unless you are both calm and composed.

Staying quiet is a coping mechanism. Silence is a form of protection and is one way in which things can go back to being normal, especially after an altercation. The one thing that you need to ask yourself before using the silent treatment is whether you are defending yourself or you are attacking someone else. If you are staying silent to manipulate your partner, then that counts as abuse. If you notice that your partner is doing the same, then it's a toxic relationship, and you are in a relationship with a manipulator.

CHAPTER TWELVE

Acceptable Manipulation

Can you manipulate someone for their own good?

There may be times when you have a strong motivation to help someone who needs your help; however, for one reason or another, they reject all your direct attempts. Maybe then, you can "manipulate" them to try and help them.

From an ethical point of view, these problems are inevitable and crucial. When in my therapeutic practice I sometimes advise clients about how they can subtly "maneuver" a child, parent, friend, or stable or highly protected professional partner to accept their well-intentioned advice or help, I often have a negative reaction. Concerned about the astuteness of my proposal, they respond, "But is this not manipulation?"

My usual answer is that their interest in having a positive influence on another person clearly seems to be sincere. So, if such a strategic approach is not for personal gain, should they really consider it to be manipulative?

English vocabulary can benefit from the addition of a new word to characterize such behavior; one that at first sight may seem dishonest or exploitative. But that, in the end, would only have a positive meaning, because the fundamental intention of the manipulator is unquestionably soft, rather than being deceitful. As such, the word I would choose as the closest synonym for such "positive manipulations" would probably be a piece of fiction. For this type of manipulation, it is a "construct," "formulation," or "plan," strategically designed to convert antagonism into cooperation, and resistance into resolution.

We all know that, sometimes, it can be very difficult to get through to someone, which reminds me of the expression, "Desperate times require desperate measures."

In this case, the "measure" is specifically designed to reduce a negative impact. Manipulators are likely to have already tried to convince the victims that they really want to help. But if all your rational attempts were left ignored, then it is entirely appropriate to use other communication tactics. Remember that your motive is not to force them to your will, but only to elude their stubborn and illogical defenses.

Here is a hypothetical example of how such "favorable" manipulations can work:

Let's say you heard of corporate rumors that your friend, a professional colleague, is at risk of being fired. A few months ago, his wife left him for another man, and he had not yet faced abandonment. In turn, he suffered from deep depression and grief, as well as a sense of boiling fury and resentment. As expected, his work deteriorated significantly. Knowing how mentally and emotionally unbalanced he was, you've already begged him to undergo treatment, or to at least take an antidepressant. But proud, angry and desperate, and denying the seriousness of his position, he obstinately rejected both options.

Since you feel like you have no other option, you think it's a good time to speak to him about your son's terrible accident a couple of years ago, and how he ended up in a coma for a couple of months before he was finally out of danger. While you are recollecting all this, you decide to stress how therapy helped you to cope with the incident.

You also talk about taking medication to help deal with your grief. If you make your friend feel like you are empathetic towards him, then the chances are that he will listen to you. You are not manipulating your friend. Instead, you are trying to convince him to do something that is good for him.

As a well-wisher, you want him to bounce back onto his feet and get on with his life. This is the primary difference between a manipulator and someone who is being persuasive. You are persuading your friend to do something that's for their own good. Even if the moving narrative that you came up with was nothing more than a lie, you are lying with a good intention.

So, it is not manipulation, and even if you want to term it as manipulation, it is acceptable in this situation.

CHAPTER THIRTEEN

Overcome Indecisiveness to Overcome Manipulation

If you want to overcome manipulation, then you need to learn to become decisive. If you are indecisive and often rely on others to help you make any decisions, then it is likely that you will be opening up doors for a manipulator to walk into your life.

Do you think you are a decisive person? Well, if you say yes immediately, then you are; however, if your answer is, "I don't know," then you probably aren't. Not many people fall in the former category. There are some who are better at decision-making than others, then there are some who can make the *right* decision more easily than others, and then there are those who need a little help in this department. Regardless of the category that you fall into, decision-making is a skill that comes in handy in every aspect of life. Being able to make good decisions is important if you want to succeed in life. Being able to make decisions quickly is equally important. We always have different options and knowing how to select one can have a serious impact on your life.

In this chapter, you will learn about the different steps that you can use to become adept at making decisions for yourself.

Don't Aim for Perfection

Stop trying to be a perfectionist.

There is nothing wrong with wanting to do your best; however, you need to know when it is the right time to stop. It doesn't mean that you must settle for less if it isn't the best. It simply means that you must set criteria and stick to it. A perfectionist always thinks, "Maybe I can do better than this" and keeps gathering information instead of acting. There will always be a different way in which you can improve upon your actions; however, you will never know if you don't try.

A perfectionist hesitates while taking the first step, which can be a major deterrent when it comes to decision-making.

Perfectionists always believe that there are only two possible outcomes in any given situation, either success or failure. This isn't how the world works, though. It is great that they want to be good at something, but it is equally important to understand where to draw the line. It's wrong to think that a task isn't completed just because it isn't perfect—this mentality can prevent you from starting something; not just starting, but even completing it. Instead of chasing perfection, focus on being better and completing the task.

Do What Franklin Did

Franklin used to make use of a method he referred to as moral algebra whenever he had to make a decision. This is a very simple yet useful technique that can help you in making decisions.

Take a piece of paper and fold it in half. On one half of it, list down the pros and on the other, write down the cons. Once you have listed everything out, strike off a pro and a con that are of equal weight. Continue to do this until there aren't any that balance; whatever is left will help you in finding a solution and help you in making a decision.

Learn to Listen to Your Inner Voice

We all have an inner voice that tries to help us in deciding what is right and wrong; however, more often than not, we tend to ignore this inner voice. We ignore it so much that it starts becoming feeble. We are all born with an instinctual compass that can help us determine what the best course of action is for us. This compass is your conscience. Whenever you think you are doing something wrong, don't you feel a sinking sensation in your gut that tells you that something is amiss?

Learn to listen to your gut.

If you have a bad feeling about something, then it probably is bad. Your intuition can guide you through a difficult decision, so learn to listen to it. In our process of growing up, we often tend to ignore our intuition because of what others say and do.

Get Rid of Bias

Perhaps one of the most clichéd questions that therapists ask their patients is, "Tell me more about your childhood."

Human beings collect their experiences and, depending on whether a particular incident or situation is positive or negative, our mind starts to create bias.

For instance, if you were ever mugged on a particular street, it is very likely that you will try to avoid that street in the future. Or perhaps you were in a relationship with an unfaithful partner—this will create trust issues and will make you question how faithful any future potential partner is. These are instances of negative cognitive bias that your brain develops. Such biases can have a lasting impact on your ability to decide.

In the same sense, your brain can favor certain things just because of the positive experience you might have had while growing up. Bias can impair your sense of decision-making and prevent you from thinking rationally.

Timing Matters

Be mindful of the specific time when you are trying to make a decision. For instance, it isn't advisable that you make a big decision after an argument with your partner. This is bound to affect your ability to think clearly, and you will end up doing something impulsively.

We often tend to make decisions when we aren't in the right frame of mind. When you are feeling angry, it is likely that you will end up doing something rashly, without thinking things through and without thinking about the repercussions of your actions. Always conclude when your mind isn't foggy; however, spending too much thinking or overanalyzing is a dangerous thing to do.

When in a bad mood, don't make a quick decision. Sleep on it or spend some time to think it through.

Importance of Things

Regardless of your age or profession, you will be faced with numerous decisions every day; however, not every decision needs to be given the same weight.

For instance, having to decide the theme for a project needs to be given more weight than deciding what you're going to have for your next meal. Learn to differentiate between the decisions that are important and the ones that aren't. You obviously shouldn't spend the same amount of time trying to research about a particular lawn fertilizer when compared to learning about a specific health condition. Learn to prioritize your tasks and spend more time while deciding something of significance.

Stay True to Yourself

Don't change yourself because someone else wants you to. Don't stray away from your faith or what you believe in just because of something or someone. Stay true to yourself; don't lose your dignity and your self-respect.

It must always be a 50/50 relationship: Don't let one person dominate you. A relationship requires compromise.

Do things that you enjoy: Don't stop doing things that you enjoy just for fitting in. Don't stop listening to your style of music or watching movies that you enjoy because those around you don't have the same tastes.

If something feels wrong, it probably is: Be kind to others and be pleasant. If you think something is wrong, then don't budge. If something doesn't feel right, it is likely that it isn't. Listen to your inner voice when in doubt. Saving your skin doesn't make you selfish and don't let someone else tell you otherwise.

Don't push yourself to network all the time: If you don't feel like networking, then don't. It is okay to take some time off for yourself; however, don't let this become a habit. Be around those who make you comfortable and with whom you can be yourself, without any pretense.

Do not, at any cost, turn to substances. Social drinking is fine, but that must be your hard limit. Don't do something just because others think it's cool. Always set boundaries in a relationship. Don't change yourself to feel accepted.

CHAPTER FOURTEEN

Stop Manipulation

Psychological manipulation is the manifestation of excessive control through emotional misrepresentation and mental exploitation with the intent of taking control, privilege, power, and benefits at the expense of the victim.

Most manipulatives have four common characteristics:

- They know how to detect your weaknesses.

- Having found the said weakness or weaknesses, they will try to use the weaknesses against you.

- With their clever machinations, they convince you to give up something of yourself to serve their selfish interests.

- When the manipulator manages to take advantage of you, it is likely that they will repeat the violation until the exploitation ends.

The fundamental causes of chronic manipulation are complex and profound. But anything that forces a person to be psychologically manipulative is not easy when you are on the verge of such aggression. How can you successfully cope with these situations?

Below are eight keys to manipulating people. Not all of these can be applied to your specific situation. Just use what works and leave the rest.

Know Your Rights

The most important rule when dealing with a person psychologically is to know their rights and recognize when they are violated. While not harming others, you have the right to defend yourself and your rights. If you harm others, you lose access to these rights. The following are few of our basic human rights:

- You have the right to be respected.
- You have the right to express your feelings, opinions, and wishes.
- You have the right to set your priorities.
- You have the right to say no without fault.
- You have the right to get what you pay for.
- You have the right to have different opinions from others.

- You have the right to take care of yourself and to protect yourself from a physical, mental or emotional threat.

- You have the right to create your happy and healthy life.

These basic human rights represent your limits. Society has many people who don't respect these rights; emotional manipulators especially deprive their victim's rights so that they can control them and use them for their benefit.

You have the control to declare that you, and not the manipulator, are responsible for your life.

Keep Your Distance

One manner in which you can easily spot a manipulator is to see if a person is acting differently in front of different people and different circumstances or social settings. While we all display a degree of this kind of social variation, some mental manipulators usually stay at the extremes, being very polite with one person and completely rude to others, or helpless in one moment and violently hostile the next. If you notice that a person's behavior seems to change rather regularly and with no prompting, then it is a good idea to maintain sufficient distance from them and avoid communicating with them.

As I mentioned earlier, the causes of chronic manipulation are complex and profound. Remember that it is not your obligation to change them. You must focus on yourself and excel in your own life.

Avoid Personalization

Since the manipulator's job is to find and use the victim's weaknesses, it is clear that you might be made to feel rather worthless or even blame yourself for not being able to satisfy the manipulator. In such situations, it is essential that you remember that you are not a problem; they are simply trying to make you feel bad, so you are more likely to give up your power and your rights.

Review your relationship with the manipulator by asking yourself the following questions:

- Do they treat you with sincere respect?
- How reasonable are the expectations and requirements of this person?
- Is this relationship one-sided or is it going both ways?

- Ultimately, does this relationship make me feel good?

Your answers to the above-mentioned questions give you the necessary clues as to whether the "problem" in this relationship is you, or not.

Concentrate on Them by Asking Questions

Unavoidably, psychological manipulators will make requests (they are not requests, but demands) from you. These "offers" usually will make you go out of your way to meet the needs and desires of the manipulator. When you hear unjustified indications, it is sometimes useful to focus again on the manipulator, asking some test questions to see if you have sufficient self-awareness to understand the injustice of your scheme. For instance:

- Does that seem sensible to you?
- Does their expectation seem reasonable and fair to you?
- Do you have anything to say in this?
- Are they asking you or telling you?
- What will you get from this?

- Do they expect you to go through with the demand?

When you ask yourself these questions, you will be able to see through the game that the manipulator is playing with you. You will be able to see that all the other person wants is to use you to get the results they want. The sooner you realize that they are exploiting you, the better.

Time is Your Friend

Manipulators often expect an answer from you immediately to show their hold and control over you in the situation. (Salespeople call this "closing the deal.") At such times, rather than responding to manipulators' demands, leverage your time, and distance yourself from them. You can take back control in such a situation by simply saying, "I'll think about it."

Consider how authoritative these few words are from a customer to a salesperson, or from a romantic prospect to an eager suitor, or from you to your manipulator. Take all the time that you need to evaluate the pros and cons of a situation, and consider whether you want to negotiate an arrangement that's suitable for you, or if you're better off by saying, "No!"

Learn to Say, "NO!"

You need to say, "No!" if you don't want to find yourself in rather troublesome situations. It is not just about saying no, but you need to be able to say it diplomatically and authoritatively.

Saying, "No!" decisively is a part of effective communication. When said the right way, it lets you stand your ground without affecting your working relationship. Remember that your fundamental human rights include the right to do what you want without having to feel guilty about it. Learning to say no is one skill that will come in handy in all aspects of your life. If you don't know how to do this, then there is no time like the present to work on this skill.

Confront the Bully

A manipulator tends to become a bully when they physically or mentally intimidate or harm someone.

The most critical thing that you need to keep in mind about aggressors is they always prey on those that they perceive to be weaker than them. So, if you seem passive and compliant to the bully then don't be surprised if you find that there's a bull's eye on your back. You effectively will be making yourself a target for the manipulator. Bullies backs off as soon as they realize that their targets can stand up for themselves and have some spine. This is true in schoolyards, as well as in domestic and office environments.

On an empathetic note, studies show that many bullies are victims of violence themselves. This in no way excuses their behavior, but it may help you consider the bully in a better light.

When confronting bullies, ensure to be in a position where you feel safe and have the ability to protect yourself. It could be standing your own ground, having others support you, or maintaining a concrete witness of the bully's inappropriate behavior.

When a manipulator vows to violate your boundaries, it is time deploy consequence. The skill in identifying and asserting consequences is one of the most important skills you can use to "stand down" a manipulative person.

The steps mentioned in this chapter are easy to follow, but you will need a little practice. So, if you no longer want to let someone else manipulate you and you want to regain control in your life, then you need to start following the information given in this chapter, today.

CHAPTER FIFTEEN

Terms and Phrases to Know

You will find manipulative people in almost all walks of life. You might bump into them at work where they take all the credit for your work or in social situations where they take the form of people who are controlling, demanding and abusive at times. Being aware of the right words to use while dealing with such people can give you the strength you need to stand up or even walk away from them. Manipulation in a romantic relationship is often a sign of an abusive relationship. So, if you feel like you are in one, my advice is to run and run fast. Once you understand these terms, it will be easier for you to see who they are, and you can gain the power to walk away from them. In this section, I will introduce you to a couple of phrases that you must know if you think you are being manipulated by someone, and what these phrases mean.

Monitoring

During the initial stages of a relationship, I am certain that you feel butterflies in your stomach, and you might know what your partner is up to at all times. However, if your partner that you are developing intimacy with is manipulative, then any love or attention that he showers on you is love bombing. If you notice that your significant other constantly wants to be in touch with you, then that's a red flag you must not ignore. Persistent texts and phone calls are a common form of stalking. Not replying to the onslaught of their messages might put you on the receiving end of your partner's excessive anger. This is another red flag that you must not ignore. You must understand that you deserve your space and anyone who doesn't respect your space and boundaries isn't worth your while.

Object Constancy

Fallouts are quite common, even more so in romantic relationships. However, manipulators like those with extreme narcissism get angry with their partners to a level that isn't acceptable. Narcissists don't have object constancy. Object constancy is the ability to retain one's positive feelings about someone while still being angry, annoyed or even disappointed. You might notice that a person like a narcissist will not feel any affection toward their partner while hurling insults or screaming at their partner. That's the primary reason why they seem like a different people altogether in such stressful situations. It is almost like they are having a Dr. Jekyll and Mr. Hyde sort of a situation.

Their reactions can be so powerful that it might make the victim feel like they were wrong. To right this alleged wrong, the submissive partner might try to alter their behavior to please the controlling partner.

Moth to a Flame

Contrary to popular belief, manipulative people don't necessarily seek out meek and submissive partners. They actively seek out prey who are strong and confident—it tends to make them feel superior. Targeting those who are vulnerable might not make a manipulator feel powerful, so they will go after someone who has the traits they like to see in themselves. They are drawn to such people like a moth to a flame.

If someone is trying to manipulate you at work, then it is perhaps because they take notice of your skills and try to look more skilled than you are.

In a relationship, they want others to know that someone as good as you have opted to be with them.

A manipulator will try to bring you down only behind the scenes, and they do this with the sole aim of breaking your confidence. By lowering your self-esteem, your partner can have better control over you, and you might also want to stick with the manipulator. Victims of a manipulative relationship often stay with their manipulators because they seem to think that it's what they deserve.

Flip the Script

Manipulators are certainly masters of smoke and mirrors. If you are a manipulator's target, then the manipulator would have studied you intensively and will be aware of all your strengths and weaknesses. These are the tools they need to possess to wind you up. Often, you might notice that they accuse you of things that they are doing or might have done.

For instance, if the manipulator cheats on you, then they might accuse you of infidelity. If they are constantly canceling your plans, then they will probably accuse you of not giving them sufficient freedom. Manipulators tend to feel quite good about themselves when they can confuse their partner and make them overly emotional.

For a manipulator, everything is a game. The only way in which you can get out of the game is to end the relationship and cut off all ties to the manipulator. At work, you need to learn to let go of the things they do and don't expect any apologies. Once they notice that you are stoic to their manipulations and that they can't rile you up, the manipulator will move on.

Gaslighting

"Gaslight" was a 1944 movie in which a man controls and tricks his wife into believing that she's losing her mind. This is where the term "gaslighting" originates from. These days, this term is used to describe the manner in which manipulators gain power over others by making them feel like they are losing their minds.

Manipulators will lie, create scenarios that never happened, but will convey it all in such a convincing manner and with such conviction, that their victims tend to believe that it's the truth. This process doesn't happen overnight. A manipulator does this slowly; it can be a small lie every now and then so that the victim doesn't see their plans of deception. It is similar to the "frog in a saucepan" analogy—

the water in the pan will be heated up slowly so that the frog doesn't realize that it is going to boil to death.

Perspecticide

A step ahead of gaslighting is percepticide. This tends to happen when a manipulator has made their victim believe so many things that are untrue, that the victim can no longer discern what's real and what's not. Whenever this happens in a romantic relationship, the victim tends to become a prisoner of their life where they aren't allowed to do anything or even think by themselves. They even give up the right to have basic beliefs related to their faith, religion and such, because of the fear they live in- of displeasing the manipulator by putting a step out of the line.

Trauma Bonds

At least from the outside, others might look at an abusive relationship and wonder how the victim managed to stick around for as long as they did. Manipulators, as well as abusive people, are quite cruel to their partners. This cruelty can be emotional, mental or even physical at times. However, they don't start like this when they are luring their victim into their trap. Manipulators tend to shower their victims with love and compliments intermittently to make them stick around. These moments occur when the partner does something or behaves in a manner that the manipulator believes to be "right or acceptable." It is a method of conditioning, and the victim unwittingly becomes accustomed to this bond of emotional push and pull.

This emotional back and forth can be quite addictive. When a person is looking for something that they desire, that they once had, which is a connection to someone they love, and the said person is playing is playing a game of cat and mouse where she is constantly pulling it back and forth, then the body develops a sort of dependency—a dependence for the manipulator's approval.

"But he didn't hit me."

Perhaps the most worrisome thing that a person who is in a toxic relationship can say is, "but he did not hit me!" Physical abuse leaves visible scars, whereas mental or psychological abuse might not leave any visible scars, but it is equally damaging. The marks of psychological abuse are harder to identify. Sadly, all manipulators are aware of this, and they tend to use this to their advantage. They realize that physical abuse is usually the breaking point for a lot of people, so they resort to such abuse that allows them absolute control over their victim without pushing them away: psychological abuse.

When people use a phrase like, "But he didn't hit me," they often mean that they will leave their partner if the said partner resorts to physical violence. Well, if you ever catch yourself saying or even thinking about this phrase, it is my honest advice that you need to move away from that relationship.

Bargaining

A manipulator never likes to lose. If the victim takes a step back or if they end the relationship, a manipulator will beg for a second chance and usually, victims tend to give in. You need to understand that manipulators might be able to change their ways for a while or even hide their ugly sides from you, but it will only be temporary. Once they think that you are pliable, they will resort to their old ways. Even if it seems like the manipulators are fighting tooth and nail to keep their victim around, it is only for their benefit. All the promises that they make are hollow and don't be surprised if they don't stick to their word.

Mental Manipulation

A manipulator always has his or her best interest in mind and no one else's.

CHAPTER SIXTEEN

Gain Payback on a Manipulator

The best revenge is to be unlike him who performed this injury—Marcus Aurelius

There will certainly be times in your life when you need to stick up for what is right and call out manipulators on their attempts to manipulate you. Whenever a manipulator seems to have overstepped, you must reset these boundaries. It is entirely up to you to pay them back in a productive manner, and no one else can do this, but you.

I am not talking about an "eye for an eye" kind of payback. The worst thing you can do is stoop down to their levels and behave like them. This passive-aggressive manner of dealing with the situation is something that manipulators will be oblivious to. If you don't do anything and if you merely let it slide by, then you are untrue to yourself. You might let something go, suck it up and tell yourself that it will not happen again.

Well, I hate to burst your bubble, but it will happen again.

Those who are used to twisting others to serve their selfish purposes without having any remorse for all the collateral damage they cause will never change their ways. This is primarily because most people don't call them out for what they are, and instead, step aside from them. This sort of behavior will silently damage your self-esteem and self-worth. If you step aside and let them have their way, they might eventually move on, and then they will start looking for new prey. At times, they might even circle back to you. All this is certainly annoying and hurtful and therefore, makes revenge seem like a good idea.

Why is revenge a bittersweet option? If you have ever been stuck with a manipulator, then you know how your thoughts about payback keep circling in your head. You don't have to feel bad while thinking about payback. It is not only normal, but it is good for your mental health. The thoughts of revenge circulating in your head are your brain's way of creating an exit strategy for you.

The thoughts of revenge will certainly make you feel good, but it is bittersweet. For instance, it ushers with it a barrage of negative emotions that remind you of your initial experiences or the offenses committed against you. The thoughts of indulging in any form of vengeful acts might provide temporary respite. Revenge-motivated aggression can be a mood enhancer, but it's not advisable.

Imagining scenarios of obtaining revenge can be a great coping mechanism, but all this leads to an increase in negative emotions that you experience. So, it might be appealing, but it isn't worth it. I believe that revenge is nothing more than a sheer waste of time.

So, how can you get revenge over manipulators?

The reality of exacting revenge is not worth your time and effort, and it will prevent you from being productive. Also, it gives the manipulator the satisfaction of gaining power over your time and attention, once again. The more you start to think about this situation, the more you are focusing on unproductive things. You are fueling the wrong beast. The real payback that you can give is to regain complete control over your life by cutting out all manipulative people from it.

When you are face-to-face with a manipulator, you need to stop talking and gossiping. Essentially, you need to stay mum. If someone tries to manipulate you, your first reaction might be to badmouth them or complain. That's not a good idea. When you turn to gossip, the only person you hurt is yourself. When you start complaining, remember that you are supplying the manipulator with more information to manipulate you further. You are essentially increasing the size of their target.

Apart from this, it will also make you seem weak and puny. The best way to give a manipulator all the control that they desire over you is by complaining. Since doing or not doing this is entirely up to you, you need to stop feeding the manipulator's need to control you.

Instead of indulging in any gossip or complaining about them, get back at the manipulator by shutting down all forms of communication with them. You don't need to give an explanation, no need to back down and you certainly don't have to rationalize your behavior. Cut them off cold turkey and don't resume communicating with them. If you don't communicate, then they can't play any of their mind games on you, and they cannot control you. If you can, then try to distance yourself from the manipulator physically.

Another thing that you can do is to become stoic. If you stay unemotional and don't respond to them in any manner, the manipulator will move on. Even if you are hurt or upset either by the acts, behavior or words of the manipulator, don't express it. If you react emotionally, you are merely making yourself weaker, and the manipulator will certainly use it against you.

If you want to get even with a manipulator, then don't let your emotions or feelings govern you. This is one thing that all manipulators prey on—emotions and feelings. Instead, you need to learn to react rationally.

If someone has tried to manipulate you or has acted in a manner that makes them untrustworthy, it is your time to act. You need to make a strategic move so that such a situation doesn't reoccur. The best manner to do this is to channel a manipulator's actions into something productive for you.

Don't indulge in any self-pity and it is not worth spilling tears over. Instead, turn this pain into a weapon. Channel this energy to make yourself productive. Growth is the best revenge that you can exact. Manipulators always need to know that their acts or behaviors have a hold over you and if you are stoic and don't let it affect you, it will quickly discourage the manipulator from manipulating you.

If you want payback, then there is one other thing that you can do, and that's to take responsibility for a situation.

Whenever a manipulator takes advantage of you, it is as much your fault as it is theirs. You are giving someone control over yourself, you put yourself in a compromising position, you never set any boundaries, and you allowed yourself to be pushed around. Now, you need to accept the responsibility for your slipups. Use the fact that you were manipulated to motivate to improve your situation.

What are your vulnerabilities? What are the aspects of your life that you want to improve and what are the skills that you need to develop?

For instance, if you notice that the manipulator gained control over you because of your indecisiveness, then learn to be decisive. If it was your low self-esteem that opened doors for manipulation, then work on improving your self-esteem.

Don't lash out on others because that's a waste of your energy. Instead, take some time for critically analyzing yourself. Make a list of all your strengths and weaknesses. Work on improving your strengths and overcoming your weaknesses.

Don't let yourself become vulnerable to manipulation ever again.

BONUS!

As an additional 'thank you' for reading this book, I want to give you another book for free. The book is:

The Simple and Powerful Word to Use to Increase Your Social Status

It's a quick read that will add a powerful tool to your psychological toolbox.

Follow the link below and you can claim the book instantly.

Click Here for Instant Access!

or go to VictorSykes.com/free-ebook

Conclusion

I want to thank you once again for purchasing this book. I hope that it proved to be insightful and informative.

Psychological and emotional manipulation is certainly not desirable, especially when you are the one who is being manipulated. Such manipulation is a blatant violation of your natural right to freedom. You are free to do as you please, as long as you don't hurt anyone else in that process.

Now that you know what mental manipulation is all about, the ways to recognize mental manipulation and the tips to overcome it, all that you need to do is apply this knowledge in your daily life.

The one thing that you must never forget is that life is unpredictable and there is very little that you can control, but the one thing that you can always control is the way you respond to a situation. Learn to listen to your gut and trust your instincts. If something doesn't feel right, then it probably isn't.

With the help of the information given in this book, you can turn your life around. You are the master of your life, and no one else has any control over you unless you let them.

Good luck!

Made in the USA
Coppell, TX
06 May 2020

24346417R00105